THE WARS OF THE ROSES 'N 100 'ACTS

MATTHEW LEWIS

AMBERLEY

First published 2017

Amberley Publishing
The Hill, Stroud
Gloucestershire, GL5 4EP

www.amberley-books.com

British Library Cataloguing in Publication Data.
A catalogue record for this book is available from the British Library.

ISBN 978 1 4456 4746 3 (paperback)
ISBN 978 1 4456 4747 0 (ebook)

Typeset in 11pt on 13pt Sabon.
Origination by Amberley Publishing.
Printed in the UK.

CONTENTS

1. The Seeds of the Wars of the Roses Were Sown in 1399

Edward III ruled England from 1327 until his death in 1377, aged sixty-four. Many historians have called him a perfect king for the combination of domestic peace and foreign glory he oversaw as the Hundred Years Wars with France began. Predeceased by his oldest son Edward, the Black Prince, by just a year, King Edward was succeeded by his grandson, Richard II, who came to the throne aged just nine.

King Richard had three surviving uncles. John of Gaunt, Duke of Lancaster, King Edward's third son, was rich and ambitious, sparking some concern that he might try and take the throne for himself. Edmund, Duke of York, and Thomas, Duke of Gloucester, also survived their father. King Edward's second son Lionel, Duke of Clarence, had died in 1368, leaving a daughter who would marry into the powerful Mortimer family.

The reign of Richard II was difficult and once he reached maturity he fell into frequent dispute with his nobles. King Richard developed a heightened sense of his own majesty – he was the first English king to adopt the appellation Your Majesty – and this led to charges of tyranny and further problems with his nobles. In 1388, a group known as the Lords Appellant tried to separate Richard from some of his favourite advisors, who they charged with corruption. Thomas, Duke of Gloucester, Thomas Beauchamp, Earl of Warwick, and Richard FitzAlan, Earl of Arundel, began the movement and were quickly joined by Henry, Earl of Derby, oldest son of John of Gaunt, and Thomas Mowbray, Earl of Nottingham. The group succeeded in their aims but King Richard harboured a deep grudge.

In 1397, having rebuilt his power base, Richard took his revenge. The three original Lords Appellant were arrested. Richard's uncle Thomas died in custody at Calais amid strong suspicion that he was killed on the king's orders. The Earl of Arundel was executed and the Earl of Warwick stripped of his lands and titles and imprisoned. The earls of Derby and Nottingham fell into dispute, each accusing the other of treason. Richard organised a trial by combat, but stopped it at the last moment and banished the men. When Derby's father, John of Gaunt, died in 1399, Richard extended his cousin's exile so that he could take the huge wealth of the Duchy of Lancaster into royal hands.

Henry was outraged and launched an invasion, landing at Ravenspur in Yorkshire. He found strong support from a nobility angered and unnerved at Richard's willingness to ride roughshod over the laws of inheritance. If he would deprive his own cousin, who would be next? Richard was forced to abdicate in favour of his cousin, who became Henry IV, the first king of the House of Lancaster. The line of succession had been broken, setting a dangerous precedent. A bad king who would not be reformed could be replaced.

2. The Death of Henry V Increased the Likelihood of Civil War

On 31 August 1422, Henry V died of dysentery on campaign in France at the age of thirty-six. Henry had only married two years earlier and left behind a son who was only nine months old to become Henry VI. The last time there had been a minority was at the beginning of the nine-year-old Richard II's reign and that had led to the House of Lancaster taking the throne just over twenty years earlier.

In order to provide for his son's minority, Henry V set out a method of government in his will. Henry had conquered swathes of France; and forced the king of France to recognise Henry as his heir. Charles VI died just weeks after his son-in-law but without an adult king to lay claim to his throne in France; England missed the opportunity Henry V had won. In England, Henry V's will provided for his youngest brother Humphrey, Duke of Gloucester, to act as regent in England. Parliament and Council quickly overturned the will, establishing the principle that a king cannot rule from beyond the grave. Instead, a three-way separation of power was created. The Earl of Warwick was given responsibility for the person of the king and for his education, the Council was to govern until the king was of age and Humphrey was created Protector of the Realm, with responsibility for the defence of England from internal and external threats. Even then, Humphrey's position was subordinate to his older brother John, Duke of Bedford, who was primarily focussed on the effort in France.

This form of rule became accepted as the norm over the following decades for minorities or circumstances in which the king was incapacitated. Henry V's will had been overridden and a division of powers and responsibility created, but this situation effectively allowed the Council supreme power to govern without reference to the king, opening the door to abuse and dispute as well as creating a problem in waiting; what would happen when the king came of age and wanted all of those powers back? Who might he blame for any problems he inherited? How were men of power to ensure that they retained that power?

Atop these problems, Henry V left a conquest of France only half completed. He had been declared heir, but Charles VI's son Charles also laid claim to the crown and controlled southern France, from where he was able, with the assistance of Joan of Arc, to launch a counter-offensive England was ill-prepared to fight. John, Duke of Bedford, worked wonders, but his resources were always limited by problems and arguments at home.

Had Henry V lived to complete his conquest and see his son grown to maturity, the problems that followed might have been avoided.

3. THE JOINING OF YORK AND MORTIMER CREATED A VIABLE ALTERNATIVE

On the death of Edward, 2nd Duke of York, at the Battle of Agincourt in 1415, his lands and titles passed to his nephew, Richard, 3rd Duke of York. Richard's father, Richard, Earl of Cambridge, had been executed for plotting against Henry V just before the Agincourt campaign began. One of the most powerful titles in the kingdom now rested with a four-year-old boy.

When Edmund Mortimer, 5th Earl of March, died in Ireland on 18 January 1425, he also left no legitimate heir. His titles and lands passed to his nephew Richard, Duke of York, whose mother Anne was Edmund's sister. As well as the prestigious and powerful dukedom, Richard now acquired vast holdings and influence in Wales, the Marches (the border region between England and Wales) and Ireland.

From his Yorkist ancestry, Richard could claim descent from the fourth son of Edward III, as opposed to the Lancastrian kings' line to the third son. However, his Mortimer heritage brought a claim to descent from the daughter of Lionel, Duke of Clarence, Edward III's second son. While royal title traditionally passed through the male line, there was no formal, codified law to govern the matter. In France, Salic Law did prevent succession through the female line, but there was no equivalent in England. In fact, Edward III had laid claim to the French crown and begun the Hundred Years' Wars based on a claim through his mother's female line.

If Edward III's logic was to be applied to the English succession, then the Mortimer claim was stronger than that of Lancaster, and the Lancastrian kings Henry IV and Henry V certainly eyed their Mortimer cousins with caution. The plot for which Richard, Earl of Cambridge, had been executed supposedly aimed to put Edmund Mortimer on the throne. Edmund's uncle, another Edmund, had been heavily involved in Owain Glyndwr's revolt in Wales and a John Mortimer was executed shortly after the infant Henry VI came to the throne.

The Mortimer claim appears to have been considered viable, even by the Lancastrian regime, and in 1425 that claim was allied to one of the most powerful noble titles in England: the dukedom of York. In the person of the teenage 3rd Duke of York, there was a viable alternative to the present king to whom the disaffected might turn in hope and treachery. The pressure upon the infant king's government to succeed was already increasing.

4. King Henry VI's Wife Did Not Inspire Fear and Hatred at the Outset

Margaret of Anjou was fifteen years old when she became Queen Consort of England, wife to the twenty-three-year-old Henry VI. During the troubles to come she was to prove the pillar of Lancastrian strength, but she was a divisive figure who also drove the parties apart. It has long been believed that she was a source of irritation, particularly to the Duke of York, from the very moment of her marriage.

One man was certainly outraged by the union. Humphrey, Duke of Gloucester, the king's uncle, protested that Henry was already contracted to marry the Duke of Armagnac's daughters and that such a vow should not be broken. Richard, Duke of York, was acting as Lieutenant-General in France at the time of the marriage and welcomed William de la Pole, Earl of Suffolk's embassy as it travelled to make the negotiations. The original intention had been to ask Charles VII for one of his daughters in marriage, but that was swiftly refused by Charles.

The compromise offered was Margaret of Anjou, a daughter of René, Duke of Anjou. René had paper claims to the kingdoms of Naples, Sicily, Aragon and Jerusalem but had bankrupted himself trying to make them a reality. He offered no dowry for his daughter beyond the promise of peace with France, an aim Henry VI had nurtured and become convinced was the correct course for England.

Richard, Duke of York, escorted Margaret through the English kingdom of France and saw her off from the coast. He offered no protest at the wedding and seems to have been involved in what took place, since as soon as Margaret was gone, he built upon groundwork laid by Suffolk for a marriage between his own son Edward and one of Charles' daughters.

The fact that Henry VI married Margaret of Anjou does not appear to have caused any great deal of upset beyond Humphrey, Duke of Gloucester's outrage at a broken promise. It was a policy that was designed to further the government's aim of peace with France, and Margaret arrived as a fifteen-year-old queen consort, unknown in England and representing a peace many by now desired. However, there were those who had an interest or belief in the continuation of war, most notably Humphrey, Duke of Gloucester, who may have resented her arrival as a sign that their faction was losing. Margaret's marriage itself did not make the Wars of the Roses inevitable. Her strength and conviction, however, may have made it more likely as the loss of focus on conflict in France and the return of settled territory there brought problems back to English shores.

5. The Start of the Wars of the Roses Can Be Dated as Early as 1447

On 14 December 1446, a summons was sent out for a parliament to open in Cambridge on 10 February 1447. On 20 January 1447, the place for the gathering was changed to Bury St Edmunds, the heartland of William de la Pole, now Duke of Suffolk, for his service to Henry VI. The reason for the late change and the new location was to cause controversy for decades to come and mark a move towards civil war.

As Humphrey, Duke of Gloucester, neared Bury, he was met by messengers of the king who ordered the duke to go straight to his lodgings and forbade him to try and contact his nephew. After two days, Humphrey was suddenly arrested. It seems that Henry VI had become convinced that his fifty-six-year-old childless uncle intended to take his throne. Two factions had emerged over the long years of Henry's minority and their opposition to each other had grown more bitter as he reached adulthood. Humphrey led a faction committed to the aims of his brother, Henry V; the complete conquest of France and the pressing of Henry's claim to the French throne. Humphrey had been at the Battle of Agincourt and had fallen in the front ranks. As French soldiers closed in to finish him off, his older brother, Henry V, stepped over him and fought them off until Humphrey could be dragged to safety. Perhaps the duke never felt able to repay this debt.

The faction opposed to Humphrey was led by Cardinal Henry Beaufort, Bishop of Winchester. The Beaufort family were also descended from John of Gaunt, as the Lancastrian kings were, but in an illegitimate line from Katherine Swynford, a line later legitimised. Cardinal Beaufort was King Henry's great-uncle and, using his income from the wealthy See of Winchester, had supported the government for decades. However, he had great trading connections and saw more profit in peace than was to be found in war. Cardinal Beaufort's nephew John had been granted the dukedom of Somerset and a free hand on a military campaign, but had failed and died on his return, leaving an infant daughter, Lady Margaret Beaufort. John's brother Edmund had, just before Christmas 1446, been given the position of Lieutenant-General of France, which had previously been held by Richard, Duke of York.

Humphrey died two days after his arrest amid rumours that he had been poisoned, though it is likely that he suffered a stroke. Humphrey was popular, as was his cause, and by his death, those dissatisfied with Henry VI's government were no longer able to focus their opposition within the House of Lancaster, on the king's uncle, who was ultimately loyal and could moderate dissent. Humphrey had identified Richard, Duke of York, as an ally. Dissent had a new focus, though the duke appears an unwilling figurehead.

6. William de la Pole's Murder Brought Civil Unrest Closer

William de la Pole, Duke of Suffolk, was exiled from England, beginning on 1 May 1450. He was convicted of minor offences, saved by the king from heavier charges of treason. Suffolk, though, never reached exile. He was intercepted in the Channel by a ship named *The Nicholas of the Tower* and beheaded. Suffolk left behind an eight-year-old son to whom he penned a letter before leaving, filled with the kind of fatherly advice Shakespeare's Polonius would expound:

My dear and only well-beloved son,
I beseech our Lord in heaven, the Maker of all the world, to bless you, and to send you ever grace to love Him and to dread Him; to the which as far as a father may charge his child, I both charge you and pray you to set all your spirits and wits to do and to know His holy laws and commandments, by which ye shall with His great mercy, pass all the great tempests and troubles of this wretched world.

And also that wittingly ye do nothing for love nor dread of any earthly creature that should displease Him. And whereas any frailty maketh you to fall, beseech His mercy soon to call you to Him again with repentance, satisfaction, and contrition of your heart, nevermore in will to offend Him.

Secondly, next Him, above all earthly things, to be true liegeman in heart, in will, in thought, in deed, unto the King, our elder, most high, and dread Sovereign Lord, to whom both ye and I be so much bound; charging you, as father can and may, rather to die than to be the contrary, or to know anything that were against the welfare and prosperity of his most royal perity of his most royal person, but that so far as your body and life may stretch, ye live and die to defend it and to let His Highness have knowledge thereof, in all the haste ye can.

Thirdly, in the same wise, I charge you, my dear son, always as ye he bounden by the commandment of God to do, to love and to worship your lady and mother: and also that ye obey always her commandments, and to believe her counsels and advices in all your works, the which dread not but shall be best and truest for you.

And if any other body would steer you to the contrary, to flee that counsel in any wise, for ye shall find it nought and evil.

Furthermore, as far as father may and can, I charge you in any wise to flee the company and counsel of proud men, of covetous men, and of flattering men the more especially; and mightily to withstand them, and not to draw nor to meddle with them, with all your might and power; and to draw to you, and to your company, good and virtuous men and such as be of good conversation and of truth, and by them shall ye never be deceived nor repent you of.

Moreover, never follow your own wit in any wise, but in all your works, of such folks as I write of above ask your advice and counsel, and doing thus, with the mercy of God, ye shall do right well, and live in right much worship and great heart's rest and ease.

And I will be to you, as good lord and father as mine heart can think.

And last of all, as heartily and as lovingly as ever father blessed his child on earth, I give you the Blessing of Our Lord, and of me, which in his infinite mercy increase you in all virtue and good living and that your blood may by His Grace from kindred to kindred multiply in this earth to His service, in such wise as after the departing from this wretched worlde here, ye and they may glorify Him eternally amongst His angels in Heaven.

Written of mine hand,
the day of my departing from this land,
Your true and loving father
SUFFOLK.

7. Jack Cade's Rebellion Offered a Warning of Trouble

In July 1450, a mysterious man calling himself Jack Cade led a large force of rebels out of Kent towards London, making camp at Blackheath. When the Duke of Suffolk's body had been found on Dover beach, the head beside it on a spike, simmering unrest boiled over. There were rumours that the king and queen meant to punish Kent for the murder and the county was already suffering problems with ships full of soldiers returning from France with no pay and no employment, leaving them to turn to crime to survive.

As Cade's group grew, the parliament in session at Leicester was hastily closed and the court moved south to London. Cade had issued a list of complaints and demands entitled 'The Complaint of the Poor Commons of Kent' and promised to await the king's answer. Henry arrived in London with around 20,000 men to be greeted by a second document known as 'The Requests by the Captain of the Great Assembly in Kent'. This document denied many of the charges, including that the Kentish men planned to remove Henry from the throne and replace him with the Duke of York, though they had called for his inclusion in government in place of those advising the king badly.

With the approach of the royal army, Cade withdrew to Sevenoaks. The king sent a portion of his force to attack the rebels, but they were defeated and the rebels lost their trust in the king. When the court fled from London back to the Midlands, it was all the incentive the force needed to march on the capital. On 2 July they reached Southwark, taking the White Hart Inn for their headquarters. On the following day they marched over London Bridge and swiftly took control of the city. On entering London, Mortimer is supposed to have struck the London stone with his knife and declared 'Now is Mortimer lord of this city!', calling himself John Mortimer. The meaning of striking the London stone, which still rests on Cannon Street, is lost, but the use of the Mortimer name transformed the revolt into a dynastic threat to the crown.

James Fiennes, Lord Say and Seale (an ancestor of the explorer Sir Ranulph Fiennes), and his son-in-law William Crowmer were executed. Both had connections to Kent and were disliked in the county. Each night, Cade led his men back to Southwark and the city left the bridge open to them to return in the morning. For three days, the rebels held the city but Cade's control began to slip. When his men turned to pillaging, the city turned against them. There was a battle on London Bridge that lasted all night, with bodies falling into the Thames. Offered a pardon, the rebels broke up and went home, but Cade's pardon was revoked and he was hunted down and killed.

Cade's Rebellion offered a warning that all was not well. It was ill-handled and no lessons were learned.

8. Henry VI Was Not Entirely Meek and Mild

Henry VI has acquired a saintly reputation as a mild-mannered man more suited to the life of a priest than that of a king, but in the aftermath of Cade's Rebellion he demonstrated that he could be vengeful and deliver the cruel justice of a medieval king.

Gregory's Chronicle is a diary kept by a resident of London up until 1469. It records that in the aftermath of Cade's Rebellion, Henry exacted revenge. Gregory noted that at Candlemas Day, 2 February 1451, Henry was at Canterbury with the dukes of Exeter and Buckingham, the Earl of Shrewsbury and other lords where four days of sessions were held to try men involved in the revolt, in spite of their pardons.

An unrecorded number of men were hanged, drawn and quartered, though they were apparently pardoned immediately after their deaths so that they could be buried whole. A further nine executions are recorded at Rochester and twelve elsewhere, all twenty-one heads displayed on London Bridge. Gregory recorded that 'Men call it in Kent the harvest of heads'. Henry VI, in spite of his piety and generally meek demeanour, was capable of delivering medieval justice, and the harvest of heads would not be the last time he would show a less merciful streak.

9. Thomas Young Paid the Price for Asking About the Succession

Parliament was abruptly closed in May 1451 when a member of the House of Commons caused controversy and outraged the king. An Act of Resumption had already been passed, taking back many of the grants made by the king in an attempt to balance his long-unbalanced books, and a petition had been presented for the rehabilitation of the reputation of Humphrey, Duke of Gloucester. It was not this, however, that caused Henry to end the session in rage.

Thomas Young MP, a member of the Commons and an apprentice at law, reportedly brought a motion forward to have Richard, Duke of York, officially recognised as Henry's heir until the king had a son of his own. The move caused the king such offence that he immediately closed the parliament and had Young arrested. In 1455, Thomas would petition to be compensated for his arrest and imprisonment, citing the parliamentary privilege of freedom of speech as his defence. He won his payment, but what he had really been trying to achieve in 1451 is not clear.

Thomas appears to have wanted York officially proclaimed heir, but what is not certain is why he did it. The obvious answer is that York arranged the motion to further strengthen his own position, but such a move was in part unnecessary, since York was already widely recognised as heir presumptive, and self-defeating, since it made York appear a clearer threat to a king who had, just four years earlier, eliminated one such threat in his uncle Humphrey.

If York was behind the bid it was perhaps in response to the inexorable rise of the Beaufort family, now led by Edmund, Duke of Somerset. Edmund was closely related to Henry and although his line had been barred from the succession by a measure that had never passed through parliament, and might easily be undone anyway. York may have feared that Somerset was manoeuvring himself into the position of heir presumptive but it would seem unwise to highlight York's own royal credentials in such an overtly assertive manner. That is not to say that York may not have acted without tact.

The motion might also have reflected a need for certainty in the country that wasn't driven by York. There was no heir remaining within the legitimate House of Lancaster. Henry VI was thirty years old and had been married for six years with no sign of a child. In seeking certainty, the finger of suspicion was directed firmly at York whether he was behind the move or not. In denying any certainty, Henry could only have been feeding the fears within the Commons that led to the request in the first place.

10. Blackheath Presented Henry VI with the Opportunity to Avoid Trouble

In 1452, Henry VI was presented with another clear notice that all was not well within his kingdom. On 9 January the Duke of York wrote to the king to complain that the Duke of Somerset was whispering against York. Whether it is true or not is hard to discern, excepting that York was out of favour and currently in a form of self-imposed exile at his castle in Ludlow. The letter was the beginning of a reassertion of York's place in politics.

On 3 February York was still at Ludlow when he wrote to towns loyal to him requesting men be sent, playing on the memory of past glory in France to draw a stark contrast to the problems he saw in the country now. York explicitly named Somerset as the cause of the troubles and explained that he meant to provide a solution. York had returned from Ireland in the wake of Cade's Rebellion to bring order but had been sidelined again when Somerset returned from France just ahead of him. As York gathered an army, it looked like there was going to be a more dangerous repeat of Cade's attack on London.

Henry and the court withdrew to the Midlands once more but York found the gates of a nervous capital closed to him. Rather than force entry, he skirted the city and set up camp at Dartford to the east. The Cottonian Roll contains an eyewitness account crediting York with 3,000 gunners and 8,000 men at arms in his centre, a further 6,000 men under the Earl of Devon to his south and 6,000 more led by Lord Cobham to the north near to seven ships on the river with their supplies. Twenty-three thousand men represented a strong force that could not be ignored.

The king sent an embassy, including York's brother-in-law Richard Neville, Earl of Salisbury, and the earl's more famous son and namesake, the Earl of Warwick, to discover York's demands. The duke insisted that he wanted only the arrest of Somerset and his removal from the king's side. When news was returned that Somerset had been seized and would face whatever charges York wished to press, the duke was elated and disbanded his force, going alone to swear his loyalty to the king again. He had been deceived. When York entered Henry's presence, Somerset stood at the king's side. Instead, it was York who was arrested, led back to London and made to swear a public oath at St Paul's never again to take up arms against the king.

York's defeat must have felt like a victory to King Henry, Queen Margaret and the Duke of Somerset, but they had ignored the warnings of a second armed uprising in two years and, in spite of York's oath, had he been dealt with more severely, or his concerns listened to more sympathetically, trouble may not have been stirred up once again.

11. The Most Expensive Medieval Jewel in England Was the Price of Failure

On 18 December 1452, Richard, Duke of York, used the most expensive jewel recorded as being in private hands in medieval England as security for a loan from Sir John Fastolf, a veteran of the wars in France and, somewhat unfairly, the inspiration for Shakespeare's comedic character Falstaff.

The loan agreement describes the jewel as 'a brooch of gold with a great pointed diamond set upon a rose enamelled white'. It was believed to have been created at the end of the fourteenth century at a cost of around 4,000 marks, over £1 million in today's money. The terms of the loan were not favourable to York, demonstrating that his wealth, particularly in his Welsh lands, was falling at the same time that he was out of favour with the king. It was a dangerous mix.

On the other hand, Henry was in the ascendant. By the beginning of 1453 there had been the first success in years in France, led by John Talbot, Earl of Shrewsbury, a famous soldier known as Old Talbot, and on top of that, Henry's queen had finally fallen pregnant, promising an heir that might end the doubt surrounding the succession. The question was whether the king could retain the upper hand.

12. Lancaster Versus York Wasn't the Only Feud in England

The Wars of the Roses is often viewed as a bitter fight between the royal houses of Lancaster and York for the throne of England, but this does not give a true impression of the situation in England as civil war edged closer. Henry VI was a weak personality and failed to perform one of the key duties of a medieval monarch in keeping feuding factions within the country in check through their shared fealty to him.

In the north of England, the ancient families of Percy, who were Earls of Northumberland, and Neville, who by this time controlled the earldoms of Salisbury and Warwick (and, via a different branch of the family, Westmorland) were at each other's throats. Both families were expanding their interests and beginning to rub up against each other. In 1453, there was a flashpoint around an inheritance issue when Thomas Neville, the second son of the Earl of Salisbury, married Maud Stanhope, giving Thomas a claim to Maud's family inheritance from Lord Cromwell. Two of the manors within that parcel were Wressle and Burwell, which had previously belonged to the Percy family before being seized when they rebelled in 1403. The loss of these manors into Neville hands was a step too far and on 24 August 1453, a party led by Thomas, Lord Egremont, the second son of the Earl of Northumberland, attacked the wedding party of Thomas Neville and Maud Stanhope. There was a skirmish, which never really came close to being a battle, at Heworth Moor but the Neville contingent were able to defend themselves as they fell back to their castle at Sheriff Hutton and it is believed that no one was killed in the fighting.

In another extremity of the realm, the Courtenay family of the Earl of Devon and the Bonville family, led by William, Lord Bonville, were causing as much trouble because of a long-standing feud in the West Country. Lord Bonville was growing in influence at Henry VI's court to the dismay of the Earl of Devon, Thomas Courtenay. The two men had fought over the lucrative stewardship of the Duchy of Cornwall and vied for supremacy across Somerset, Devon and Cornwall. In 1451, the Earl of Devon had laid siege to Taunton Castle so that York had been forced to march into the region and enforce peace. As Bonville grew in favour at court, the Earl of Devon became allied to Richard, Duke of York, joining his force at Dartford in 1452. Failure there only swung the balance further in Bonville's favour.

With Henry unable to force these factions to unite around him, the disputes became more bitter. In 1453, the Duke of Somerset and the Earl of Warwick also quarrelled over the inheritance of Cardiff Castle and, as Somerset gathered an army to attack Warwick, Henry set out west from London to try and deal with the matter, but the stress was beginning to show as he fell ill.

13. HENRY VI SUFFERED BOUTS OF MENTAL ILLNESS

The year 1453 had begun well for Henry VI. His wife was pregnant after eight years of marriage and Richard, Duke of York, had been put in his place at Dartford. However, as feuds around the country threatened to run out of control, Henry finally decided to intervene on behalf of his favourite courtier, Edmund, Duke of Somerset, who was in dispute over ownership of Cardiff Castle with Richard Neville, the Earl of Warwick, later remembered as The Kingmaker. Henry had taken Somerset's side in the dispute and was travelling west to try and bring the powerful men to terms.

In early August, Henry arrived at the royal hunting lodge of Clarendon in Wiltshire. The king was suddenly and unexpectedly struck down by illness and left in a catatonic state. *Benet's Chronicle* asserted that Henry was 'so incapable that he was neither able to walk upon his feet nor to lift up his head'. Medicine at this time still centred around the ancient Greek notion of the four humours – blood, phlegm, yellow bile and black bile – which had to be kept in balance to maintain a healthy body. Henry's physicians treated him with a variety of poultices, bleedings and medicinal draughts but to no avail.

Henry remained catatonic, having to be fed and carried from place to place, for over a year, during which government in his name became impossible. The problem could no longer be hidden when John Kemp, the Archbishop of Canterbury, died, since the king was required to appoint his replacement. The council turned to the previously disgraced Richard, Duke of York, to offer a lead. In what was considered something of a miracle, Henry made a sudden and unexpected recovery on Christmas Day 1454. He would be withdrawn from government again in 1455, though it is unclear whether he was really ill again at this point, but weakness dogged him for the rest of his life.

A diagnosis of Henry's condition at such a distance is difficult. It has been suggested that he suffered bouts of catatonic schizophrenia and depression. His maternal grandfather, Charles VI of France, was known as Charles the Mad and had frequent debilitating breakdowns, often refusing to wash, deal with state business and sometimes believing himself to be made of glass so that he was terrified he might shatter if he was touched. He had even killed members of his court in a panicked frenzy when frightened that he was about to be smashed. It seems likely that Henry inherited something of his grandfather's illness, though stress may well have played a huge part too. In July 1453, England lost the Battle of Castillon, the last great battle of the Hundred Years' Wars and with it, all territory and hope in France except for Calais. The impact of this, along with the numerous ongoing feuds demanding Henry's attention all at the same time, may have contributed in bringing out the illness that afflicted not only him, but also the country.

14. The Paston Letters Reveal Medieval Misogyny in Government

The Paston family were a gentry family from Norfolk who became wealthy and prominent in their region during the fifteenth century. Uniquely, correspondence between the family and their various contacts was retained by the Pastons and survives to the present day. The collection provides a fascinating and valuable insight into late medieval family life, local and national politics and the daily business of the landed gentry.

In 1454, the Paston Letters offer a telling glimpse at the misogyny that existed at the very pinnacle of English society. As it became clear that Henry VI's debilitating illness could no longer be kept a secret, the Paston Letters record that in January 1454, Henry's French queen, Margaret of Anjou, staked a claim to the power of a regent in her husband's name:

> Item, the queen hath made a bill of five articles, whereof the first is, that she desireth to have the whole rule of this land, the second, that she may make the chancellor, treasurer, the privy seal, and all other offices of this land, with sheriffs, and all that the king should make; the third, that she may give all the bishoprics of this land, and all other benefices belonging to the king's gift; the fourth is, that she may have sufficient livelihood assigned her for the king, the prince, and herself; but as for the fifth article, I cannot yet know what it is.

Margaret demanded not only the right to rule in the name of her husband but also to protect the rights of her son, the infant Prince Edward, who had been born on 13 October 1453. The queen by now feared the intentions of the Duke of York. Her concern was only increased as

York attracted the support of the Neville family, alienated by Henry's favouring of Somerset in their dispute over Cardiff Castle.

The queen's bid for authority caused terrified and perhaps even confused consternation among the men of power in England who simply could not comprehend the idea of a woman holding and exercising the authority of a man. Rather than submit to a woman, the council took the only other viable option and appointed Richard, Duke of York, as Protector of the Realm and gave him a prominent position within the government. Although many in the government were aware of the suspicion surrounding York, it appears from the Paston Letters and their subsequent actions that these powerful men simply could not envisage a woman at the head of the government of England and preferred the risk presented by handing power to York.

15. THE DUKE OF YORK'S FIRST PROTECTORATE WAS AN INCLUSIVE GOVERNMENT

When Richard, Duke of York, presided over his first council meeting as Protector of the Realm on 30 March 1454, following his appointment three days earlier, the composition of the council must have allayed some of the fears of those afraid of York's intentions. Although allies such as Richard Neville, Earl of Salisbury, and his son Richard, Earl of Warwick, sat along with Henry Bourchier, who was married to York's aunt Isabel, and John Tiptoft, Earl of Worcester, there were less likely figures around the table too.

Humphrey Stafford, Duke of Buckingham, was a firm member of the court party and lords Scales, Beaumont, Dudley and Fiennes were not sympathetic to York. It may have helped to alleviate fears that York had allowed a bill through Parliament on 15 March, just prior to his appointment, formerly creating King Henry's infant son Edward as Prince of Wales. York was already the King's Lieutenant in Parliament, so the bill must have had his consent if not originated from him. Until the king formerly recognised his son, the baby's position was not certain, but York put that issue to bed despite Henry's inability to acknowledge his son, surely hoping to also remove fears about his own designs on the throne.

In November a new set of ordinances to govern the household of the king, queen and prince were enacted in an attempt to bring down the rocketing costs of running them. The ordinances set out to restore the size and cost of the royal household to that operated by the king's father, Henry V, but included a provision for the king's half-brothers Edmund and Jasper Tudor to be included in the group to attend upon the king. Queen Margaret was reportedly outraged by what she saw as restrictions placed on her by York, increasing her concern about his motives despite the inclusive nature of his government.

On Christmas Day 1454, as quickly as he had fallen ill, Henry recovered. The council had been making provision for government in Henry's name until his son Edward came of age, such was the concern among the royal physicians that the king would never recover. On 9 February 1455, Henry was well enough to attend Parliament and formally bring an end to the Duke of York's protectorate. On 4 March, Edmund Beaufort, Duke of Somerset, was freed from the Tower on the king's orders. Somerset loudly protested his innocence in Parliament and complained that he had been detained for over a year without charge. Henry cleared him of any wrongdoing and referred the dispute between York and Somerset to the arbitration of eight lords.

Many of the provisions of York's time in government were immediately undone, offices given to him and his allies were taken back and he was excluded from the next council that met. Somerset resumed his place at Henry's right hand and tension grew once more.

16. The First Battle of St Albans Was Not a Dynastic Dispute

The beginning of the Wars of the Roses is consistently dated to 22 May 1455 when the First Battle of St Albans took place. This battle is striking for several reasons, including the fact that it took place in the streets of the town rather than in a field outside, which was the norm. However, it would be incorrect to classify this battle as part of the dynastic fighting between Lancaster and York that would follow some years later.

Richard, Duke of York, and his ally Richard Neville, Earl of Salisbury, had not been summoned to another council meeting at Westminster early in 1455 when both men, along with Salisbury's son, Richard Neville, Earl of Warwick, were called to a Great Council at Leicester, which was to open on 21 April 1455. Much of the power base of the House of Lancaster was not focussed around the town (now city) of Lancaster but rather covered a broad belt across the East Midlands focussed on the region around Coventry, Leicester and Kenilworth. The previously excluded lords seem to have been instantly suspicious of their summons into the heart of Henry's lands, perhaps remembering the fate of Humphrey, Duke of Gloucester, in 1447. The court party was no doubt equally fearful when the lords declined the summons and began to muster an army.

On 20 May York, Salisbury and Warwick were at Royston, just south of Cambridge, when Richard wrote to Thomas Bourchier, Archbishop of Canterbury, to insist that he meant no disloyalty to Henry. The following day York wrote directly to the king from Ware, complaining of 'our enemies of approved experience, such as abide and keep themselves under the wing of your Majesty Royal' in a clear reference to Somerset. Richard continued that they were coming to Henry as his 'true and humble liege men' and voiced concern that he had received no response to his letter to the Archbishop of Canterbury, which he had asked to be forwarded to the king. Both letters had apparently been intercepted by Somerset and had not reached the king.

As morning broke on 22 May, York, Salisbury, Warwick and their army of around 6,000 men stood in Key Fields just outside the eastern gate of St Albans, where the king was securely barricaded inside. York sent a further message to the king – an ultimatum. He wanted Somerset handed over into his custody and he would accept nothing less. Having learned a painful lesson at Dartford in 1452, York wrote 'we will not cease for any such promise, surety, nor other, until we have him which have deserved death, or else we do die therefore'.

The battle that followed was not over Henry's crown. York offered no challenge to that right. The fight was for the right to be Henry's chief advisor; it was a personal battle between York and Somerset.

17. The Daring Earl of Warwick Broke the Deadlock at the First Battle of St Albans

After three hours of negotiations saw no progress on the morning of 22 May 1455, the Duke of York and the earls of Salisbury and Warwick attacked the barricades thrown up around the town. York and Salisbury attacked the gates, guarded for the king by Lord Clifford, and could find no way through. The Earl of Warwick finally made an important breakthrough that changed the course of the battle.

While scouting the outside of the defences, a weak point was spotted and Warwick's force was able to break into gardens at the back of buildings on Holwell Street. The earl's men swarmed through the narrow streets towards the market square where King Henry stood beneath his royal banner wearing full armour and surrounded by the dukes of Somerset and Buckingham and their men. The force was not fully prepared, unaware that their outer defences had been breached, and was taken completely by surprise as trumpets blasted and cries of 'A Warwick! A Warwick!' went up.

As Warwick's archers rained down arrows, there was panic. Those on the barricades heard the trumpets and cries and ran back into the town to find out what was happening. This brought a weakening of the barricades that allowed York and Salisbury to break through and move up through the town towards the market square. In the chaos that followed in the streets of St Albans, the Duke of Somerset, the Earl of Northumberland and Lord Clifford were killed, King Henry and the Duke of Buckingham were among the injured and many soldiers lay dead in the tight streets of the town.

Casualties were not recorded as being high, perhaps as low as a hundred men, but in the confines of the town, it must have appeared far worse. John Whethamstede, the abbot of St Albans, recorded in his chronicle the shock that he felt at seeing the aftermath of the fighting. He wrote that 'here you saw a man with his brains dashed out, here one with a broken arm, another with his throat cut, a fourth with a pierced chest'.

On the day after the battle, Henry, having received medical treatment, was escorted back to London, entering the capital in majesty with York and Salisbury riding at his sides and Warwick carrying the sword of state before the king. Although Henry unquestionably remained king, it was clear that there was a new power at his side to replace Somerset. Warwick's prominent position was a reward for the daring and decisive role that he had played in the Yorkist victory at the First Battle of St Albans, but this was not yet a conflict for the crown of England.

18. James Butler, Earl of Wiltshire, Was Too Handsome to Fight

James Butler was the 1st Earl of Wiltshire and 5th Earl of Ormond, from a powerful Irish noble family. He was considered a very good looking man. In fact, he was so good looking that it hampered his performance on the battlefield.

James rose to prominence in Henry VI's service, receiving the earldom of Wiltshire as a reward. He fought in the king's army at the First Battle of St Albans on 22 May 1455 while in his early thirties. Although on the losing side, with many of his senior comrades killed or injured, James made good his escape from the town. *Gregory's Chronicle*, kept during the build-up to and early outbreak of the Wars of the Roses by a London merchant, quipped that James had 'fought mainly with his heels for he was frightened of losing his beauty'.

Despite abandoning the king's banner at St Albans, James had the audacity to write to the Duke of York from Petersfield to ask for permission to return to the king's side, or, failing that, to be allowed to return to his Irish lands. Bulter would be on the losing side at the later battles of Mortimer's Cross in 1460 and Towton in 1461, following which he was captured and executed, his good looks finally lost for the Lancastrian cause.

19. The Percy/Neville Feud Was Escalated at the First Battle of St Albans

One of the key features during the build-up of the civil war in England was the number and ferocity of local feuds that began to escalate onto the national stage. The Courtenay/Bonville feud in the south-west was bitter but matched by the Percy/Neville feud in the far north. There had already been a conflict at Heworth Moor and the Neville family, led by the Earl of Salisbury, had become attached to the cause of Salisbury's brother-in-law Richard, Duke of York, who was married to the earl's sister Cecily.

The Percy family were close to Somerset and the king, setting them further at odds with their Neville foes and at the First Battle of St Albans their feud reached the national stage. Henry Percy, Earl of Northumberland, was within the town of St Albans with King Henry and the Neville earls of Salisbury and Warwick were prominent within York's force. When Warwick broke the deadlock and enabled York and Salisbury to enter the town, the Earl of Northumberland, who was by then in his early sixties, was among those killed before the fighting ended.

The Neville family surely counted this as a crucial victory in their personal feud with the Percy family. Salisbury was in his mid-fifties and his son Warwick was twenty-seven when they helped the forty-three-year-old Duke of York to victory. The problem was that the First Battle of St Albans did not end the feuding, but only intensified it. The Earl of Northumberland's sons, including Henry, the new earl, and Thomas, Lord Egremont, were determined to avenge their father's death. Lord Clifford's twenty-year-old son John swore that he would have revenge on those who had killed his father. The nineteen-year-old Henry Beaufort, son and heir to the Duke of Somerset, was also injured at St Albans and wanted restitution for what he viewed as the murder of his father.

Although the First Battle of St Albans did not represent the beginning of a dynastic conflict for the throne of England, it did mark a sharp intensification of the feuds running out of control across England. The Yorkist party had gained the upper hand over the court party championed by Somerset and Queen Margaret. The Neville earls had defeated their Percy rivals but York's previous period in the ascendant had been dramatically cut short and nothing was certain as they rode into London the following day. Nothing, that is, except that it was not over. The sons of St Albans wanted their revenge.

20. KING HENRY COULD HAVE DIED AT THE FIRST BATTLE OF ST ALBANS

During the First Battle of St Albans, as Warwick's archers fired at the men defending the king, Henry VI was struck by an arrow that cut him on the neck. As the fighting grew closer, the king was taken into a tanner's shop to receive treatment and to keep him out of the way of further harm.

Benet's Chronicle records that once the battle was won, York, Salisbury and Warwick burst into the tanner's shop and found Henry, wounded and at their mercy. Instead of finishing off the king, as York might have done had he truly wanted the crown by this stage, *Benet's Chronicle* explains that the lords fell to their knees and pledged their allegiance to the king, 'at which he was greatly cheered'.

Henry was escorted to the comfort of the abbey to continue his treatment and, although he was dismayed to learn of Somerset's death, he was well treated and on the following morning he was escorted to London by the Yorkist lords. York might well have widened the wound at Henry's neck and ensured that there were no witnesses. He could then have blamed the stray arrow for killing the king. This is possibly the clearest sign that at this point, Henry's crown was safe and secure.

21. A Fortune Teller Had Warned the Duke of Somerset of How He Would Die

Edmund Beaufort, Duke of Somerset, had supposedly received a prophesy from a fortune teller at a local fair when he was young. The prophesy had warned that he would meet his death beneath the castle.

Edmund reportedly developed a belief that the castle referred to was Windsor Castle, and thus avoided the area for fear of the prophesy. During the First Battle of St Albans, it is believed that Somerset and his men were backed into an inn and made a desperate attempt to push out through their attackers. Edmund is believed to have fallen fighting bravely and when he fell, he might have noticed that the sign above his head was that of The Castle Inn.

If the prophesy was real, then Edmund had been mistaken to fear Windsor Castle and might never have guessed that it referred to an inn.

22. It Is Not Clear That Henry VI Was Ill During the Second Protectorate

Following the First Battle of St Albans, the Yorkist party had control of the king and government once more. The Duke of Buckingham, according to the Paston Letters, came to the Duke of York, his brother-in-law, and swore 'that he shall be ruled'. Parliament was opened on 9 July 1455 in King Henry's presence before he was taken to Hertford Castle. John Paston wrote that it was a nervous affair, noting that 'Some men hold it right strange to be in this parliament and me thinketh they be wise men that do so'. The Yorkist lords used this first session to try and protect themselves from repercussions of what was, in reality, their treason at St Albans, enacting that none of them should be 'impeached, sued, vexed, hurt or molested in their bodies, goods or lands' for their involvement in the battle. The rehabilitation of the reputation of Humphrey, Duke of Gloucester, was also a key concern of this Parliament.

When the second session of this Parliament began on 12 November, the king was absent for what the Parliament Rolls record as 'certain, just and reasonable causes'. It has long been assumed that this meant that Henry's health had failed once more, but there is no evidence beyond rumour and assumption to support that belief. The Paston Letters record only that 'some men are afraid that he is sick again' but the Commons were quick to request York's reappointment as Protector of the Realm. The delegation submitting the request was led by William Burley, a man with connections to the Duke of York, and the Commons would not conduct any business until they received an answer to their request.

It is possible that York felt too restricted and that his position was too fragile without the powers of a protector and the position at the head of the council that had allowed him to operate so decisively in 1454. When the Lords acquiesced, York set out several conditions before he would agree to take the role, including the recording of the fact that he had not sought the role, no doubt as a protection against future accusations of grasping at power, and a suitable wage for the role along with the payment of 2,000 marks he was owed for his previous time as protector.

Appointed on 18 November 1455, the second protectorate lasted only three months, being ended on 25 February 1456. King Henry suddenly appeared in Parliament to take back control, though the move followed an attempt to process an act of resumption designed to aid crown finances, but which would have deprived many who had gained under Henry's feeble leadership. Henry seemed reinvigorated, beginning a royal progress around his kingdom. York can have been in little doubt that his position was once again dangerously fragile.

23. Henry VI Summoned a Great Council to Resolve the Disputes in England

Following the end of the second protectorate, Henry VI seems to have been increasingly happy to leave the government of the realm to his wife, Queen Margaret, and the court party that surrounded her, which had at its core the sons of those nobles killed at the First Battle of St Albans. However, the growing tension within the kingdom did finally pierce the king's cocoon and demand his attention.

In January 1458, a Great Council was called to sit in London and York, Salisbury and Warwick were summoned. The aim of the meeting was to resolve the disputes driving a wedge between powerful elements in the country. York arrived in the capital with 400 men, Salisbury with 500 and Warwick sailed over from Calais with 600. Somerset brought 800 men with him while Northumberland, Lord Egremont and Lord Clifford arrived with a total of 1,500 men at their backs. The Yorkist lords were lodged within the city walls and the court party's lords outside as the mayor mobilised 5,000 citizens each day and 3,000 each night to try and keep the peace in the melting pot that threatened to boil over.

Two months of intense negotiations followed, led personally by the king with the assistance of Thomas Bourchier, Archbishop of Canterbury. No record of those talks remains, but they must have been tense, with hot-blooded men on both sides feeling that they were the wronged party. On 24 March 1458, the results of the long negotiations were published. The matter was to be settled by reparations for the deaths at the First Battle of St Albans. York was required to pay the family of Edmund Beaufort, Duke of Somerset, 5,000 marks, though he was permitted to reassign money owed to him by the Exchequer (which he might have felt he would never see anyway). Warwick was ordered to pay Lord Clifford 1,000 marks and Salisbury was instructed to cancel fines owed to him by the Percy family. The three Yorkist lords were also required to endow St Albans Abbey with £45 per year to pay for prayers for those killed in the battle.

The court party got off relatively lightly. Lord Egremont was deemed the chief troublemaker on that side and was bound over for 4,000 marks to keep the peace with the Neville family for ten years. The settlement placed the Yorkist lords firmly in the wrong, but they did not baulk at the arrangements. The king was understandably thrilled at the outcome and seemed to genuinely believe he had found a solution. He was unable to see beyond the façade his lords offered, even when the young nobles of the court party ambushed York during the negotiations.

24. HENRY VI PARADED HIS PEACE ON A LOVE DAY

On the same day as the results of Henry VI's settlement between his feuding nobles was published, 24 March 1458, the triumphant king organised a procession through the capital city to St Paul's Cathedral, which became known as the Love Day.

King Henry led the parade, wearing his crown. Behind him walked his wife, Queen Margaret, holding hands with Richard, Duke of York. Following them was Richard Neville, Earl of Salisbury, holding hands with Henry Beaufort, Duke of Somerset. Next, Salisbury's son Richard Neville, Earl of Warwick, walked hand in hand with either the Duke of Exeter or the Earl of Northumberland, the sources becoming unclear at this point. As king, Henry represented the one common thread between these factions and the only hope of uniting them.

John Lydgate wrote a poem to praise the peace and the display of unity called 'Upon The Reconciliation Of The Lords Of The Yorkist Faction With The King And His Adherents' in which he also warned France and Brittany that a united England would be looking across the Channel once again. Over a century later, with the benefit of hindsight, the Tudor antiquary Richard Grafton wrote 'For their bodies were joined by hand in hand, whose hearts were far asunder: their mouths lovingly smiled, whose courages were enflamed with malice: their words were sweet as sugar, and their thoughts were all envenomed.'

It seems unlikely that anyone involved in the display of unity other than the king himself believed that it was true. What the crowds that gathered to watch it thought is hard to know. Perhaps they hoped there might be peace without really buying the pageant. Either way, the two sides soon retreated to their corners and little seemed to really change.

The delusional Henry might have been pleased and believed that he had settled the feuding. York appeared to take his bitter medicine, but was still in the political wilderness. Queen Margaret endured holding the hand of a man she was increasingly convinced wanted her husband's throne and her young son's inheritance, but she continued to draw the young sons of St Albans close about her. As the Love Day ended, peace was no closer but remained as out of reach as ever.

25. The Peace Was Broken at Blore Heath With the Help of a Friar and a Cannon

Queen Margaret was in Cheshire when reports reached her that the Earl of Salisbury had marched out of his family seat at Middleham Castle, Yorkshire, with somewhere between 3,000 and 6,000 men. Margaret called upon a veteran of the wars in France, James Tuchet, Lord Audley, and despatched him with a force of between 6,000 and 12,000 men to intercept Salisbury, who was heading for York's stronghold at Ludlow.

On the morning of St Tecla's Day, Sunday 23 September 1459, Lord Audley laid out his larger force across Blore Heath near to the border between Staffordshire and Shropshire. The broad, open space of the heath suited the large contingent of mounted men in Lord Audley's army. Salisbury's scouts spotted the large force trying to hide behind hedgerows and the earl, himself a former soldier in France, ordered spikes to be dug into the ground to guard against a cavalry charge. He had a thick wood on his left flank for protection, but his right and rear were open. With further reports of another army loyal to the queen within 10 miles, Salisbury ordered a defensive ditch to be dug at his rear and protected his right flank with his baggage train. The wily earl had also ensured that a narrow but deep brook separated the armies just beyond bow range.

Audley ordered his men to advance and archers on both sides opened fire, causing a handful of casualties on Salisbury's side but killing or injuring around 500 of Audley's men. Lord Audley drew back, but soon ordered another charge. Salisbury's men began to flee but as the cavalry charge gathered pace, they turned and opened fire again. The withdrawal had been a trick and around 100 of Lord Audley's men fell, possibly including the baron himself at this point.

Lord Dudley, Audley's second in command, ordered his men to dismount and charge across the brook, and hand-to-hand fighting was fierce for around half an hour. Eventually, Dudley was pushed back and many men were killed trying to get back across the brook, which reportedly ran red with the blood of the fallen for miles downstream for three days after the battle.

The Earl of Salisbury gathered his force and marched on to Ludlow. Remembering the reports of another nearby force, he left one of his cannon behind and paid a friar to continually fire it all night to try and confuse the force searching for them as darkness fell and trick them into thinking the battle was still going on. Under that cover, Salisbury reached Ludlow safely and joined the Duke of York.

26. THE FIRST RECORDED GATHERING OF THE SONS OF YORK WAS AT LUDLOW IN 1459

As tensions mounted during 1459, Richard, Duke of York, had moved his family from their seat at Fotheringhay Castle in Northamptonshire to the more defensible fortress at Ludlow on the border with Wales in the heart of the Mortimer lands that he had inherited from his uncle Edmund.

Richard's wife Cecily brought with her their remaining unmarried daughter, Margaret, who was thirteen (the couple's other two daughters were already married, the twenty-year-old Anne to the Duke of Exeter and the fifteen-year-old Elizabeth to John de la Pole, Duke of Suffolk). Their two young sons, George, aged nine, and Richard, who was six, also came to Ludlow and were joined by their older brothers, the seventeen-year-old Edward, Earl of March, and the sixteen-year-old Edmund, Earl of Rutland.

Although it is possible that the large family had been together before this, their arrival at Ludlow is the first time they can be confidently pinpointed in the same place at the same time. Two of the sons of York would become kings of England as Edward IV and Richard III, but before then, they were brothers, perhaps meeting all together for the first time on the brink of war.

27. There Was No Battle at the Battle of Ludford Bridge

At the beginning of October 1459, the Duke of York and his army marched out of Ludlow, heading for London, much as he had done in 1452. As they passed Worcester, scouts returned with worrying news. King Henry himself was riding at the head of a much larger army than they had, flying the royal banner. York fell back to Worcester where he took Mass at the cathedral and swore an oath of allegiance to the king before the bishop. Then, he marched his men all the way back to Ludlow where they began to throw up defences around the fields outside the town near to Ludford Bridge.

Late in the evening on 12 October, the royal army came into view and set up camp, ensuring that the royal banners could be seen flying. Richard Beauchamp, Bishop of Salisbury, was sent to offer the king's terms to the rebels. Henry offered to pardon all except Salisbury and a few others involved at Blore Heath because of their attack on his queen's army. This made the deal unpalatable to the Yorkist lords and was perhaps meant to divide them or see them condemned together.

It was reported that Yorkist cannons fired into the darkness, though a night-time bombardment was never likely to be accurate. It was also reported that York spread a rumour that King Henry was already dead and caused Mass to be said for his soul, which, if true, was against the Church's law. There can be little doubt that there was panic in the Yorkist camp. Andrew Trollope, leader of the Calais garrison members that Warwick had brought with him, scaled the earthworks and took his men into the safety of the king's pardon. The Calais garrison was the closest thing to a professional army in

England at the time and apart from the loss of men, they took information about the defences with them too.

York, March, Rutland, Salisbury and Warwick left the camp for an emergency council of war in Ludlow Castle. When the sun rose the next morning, they were nowhere to be seen. Standing and fighting risked losing with men unwilling to fight the king. Surrender might have led to more embarrassment, if not execution. York had taken his son Rutland and made for Ireland while March, Salisbury and Warwick headed south for the safety of Calais. York left his wife and three younger children behind to be taken into royal custody as the king allowed his men to ransack Ludlow for its loyalty to York. *Gregory's Chronicle* recorded that they 'went wet-shod in wine, and then they robbed the town, and bore away bedding, clothe, and other stuff, and defouled many women' in an episode that brought little glory to the victors.

28. The Parliament of Devils Made the Civil War a Dynastic Struggle

Writs were issued on 9 October, before the Battle of Ludford Bridge, for a Parliament to open on 20 November 1459 in Coventry, the heart of Henry VI's power base. The session was later dubbed the Parliament of Devils for its savage attack on the Yorkist lords and marks the transformation of the civil war and feuding into a dynastic struggle for the throne of England.

The Parliament Rolls detail the trouble caused by the Duke of York, going all the way back to Cade's Rebellion in 1450, bringing up the First Battle of St Albans as well as Blore Heath and Ludford Bridge to show that York had been destabilising government for years. Henry granted a petition that requested the attainder of York, Salisbury, Warwick and many others.

An attainder was the highest form of punishment, particularly for a noble family. It was rarely used before the Wars of the Roses but became increasingly prominent in the power struggles. Parliament was used as a court of law but required no evidence and offered no option for mounting a defence. The king could enact a guilty verdict that meant all lands, titles and properties of the guilty party were forfeited to the crown and their children and future descendants were also deprived of everything. For a noble family, it was devastating unless it might be later undone. For the most powerful noble in the land, the Duke of York, it was catastrophic.

York was in Ireland with his son Edmund. Salisbury and Warwick were in Calais with York's oldest son Edward. All were effectively landless commoners and were convicted of treason. Three dukes, five earls, twenty-four other lords, both archbishops and sixteen bishops gave an oath of loyalty to Henry VI, his queen and his son as part of the Parliament's business too.

The Parliament of Devils left the Yorkist lords under no illusion that their cause was utterly destroyed. It also left them with nothing more to lose. Warwick made a trip from Calais to Ireland to collect his mother, who had travelled with York, in March 1460. It is not known what the duke and earl might have discussed, but they may have agreed a course of action that would end in a challenge to Henry VI for the right of the Lancastrian kings to wear the crown of England.

29. Thomas, Lord Stanley, Had a Lucky Escape in 1459

When Parliament met in November 1459, there was much to deal with in the aftermath of the battles of Blore Heath and Ludford Bridge, but one small piece of business was recorded that might have radically altered the course of the Wars of the Roses.

At the very end of the Parliament Rolls there is a request from the Commons for Thomas, Lord Stanley, to be attainted for treason. The petition states that Stanley had been summoned to the king at Nottingham but failed to attend and that his brother, William Stanley, had joined Salisbury's army, taking with him many of Thomas's servants.

Several other accusations were made against Lord Stanley but King Henry deferred consideration of them for another time, perhaps in an early acknowledgement of the power he wielded in the number of men he could raise. Given Lord Stanley's later prominent and decisive role in the Wars of the Roses, the conflict might have looked very different if this request to attaint him for treason had been acted on.

30. A Raid on Sandwich Led to an Awkward First Meeting of Future Family

In January 1460, a royal fleet was being gathered on the south coast to attack Calais and drive out the earls of March, Salisbury and Warwick. The Duke of Somerset had been made Captain of Calais in Warwick's place, but could not force the Yorkist lords out. Warwick, his fame as a daredevil increasing all the time, had no intention of sitting and waiting for an attack.

Sir John Denham was sent across the channel with around 800 men to see what was going on. He managed to arrive under cover of night and rather than scouting the royalist position, he decided to attack and took them by surprise. As at Ludford Bridge, there was little if any actual fighting. Instead, Denham managed to steal the bulk of the royal ships and capture the man sent to take charge of the preparations. Richard Woodville, Lord Rivers, was taken from his bed as he slept, as was his twenty-year-old son Anthony. Denham returned to Calais with the ships and his prisoners in tow.

Richard Woodville's father had been a chamberlain to the king's uncle John, Duke of Bedford, and after the duke's death, Richard had married his widow, Jacquetta of Luxembourg. The social mismatch had caused a scandal but Richard received a barony to give the marriage a semblance of dignity. The Paston Letters record that the father and son were hauled before the earls of March, Salisbury and Warwick to be teased:

And there my Lord of Salisbury rated him, calling him a knave's son, that he should be so rude to call him and these other lords traitors, for they all shall be found the king's true liege men, when he should be found a traitor. And my Lord of Warwick rated him, and said that his father was but a squire, and brought up with King Henry the Vth, and sithen himself made by marriage, and also made lord, and that it was not his part to have such language of lords, being of the king's blood. And my Lord of March rated him in like wise. And Sir Anthony was rated for his language of all three lords in like wise.

Edward, Earl of March, would go on to marry Richard Woodville's daughter, Anthony's sister Elizabeth. This first meeting in which Edward berated his future father-in-law and brother-in-law as low-born men must have made it awkward when it was time to meet his wife's family.

31. Lord Scales Used Wildfire Against the People of London

On 26 March 1460, Warwick landed at Sandwich with a force of 2,000 men and accompanied by his father Salisbury and the young Edward, Earl of March. The invading force was well received and their numbers increased as they moved north to London.

Warwick was popular, particularly in the capital where he frequently spent vast amounts of money with merchants, who also appreciated his efforts to keep the Channel free of pirates. Lords Scales and Hungerford were the senior royal representatives in the capital at the time, with the king still in his heartlands in the Midlands. They ordered the city gates closed and barred as Warwick approached, but they were roundly ignored and the large force was welcomed into London like liberators.

Lord Scales was a veteran of campaigns in France and had held the Tower of London during Jack Cade's attack on the city. In his mid-sixties, Lord Scales reacted so strongly to the threat that it would cost him his life. As Warwick's men, their numbers increased by Kentish men and citizens of London, approached the Tower, Lord Scales ordered the fortress's artillery to open fire into the crowd. Gun stones hurtled into the crowd as cannons cracked angrily. Lord Scales went further, though, and unleashed a terrible, deadly weapon on the crowd. The Byzantine Empire had called it Greek fire, but in England it was known as Wildfire. The precise recipe had been lost but the closest modern parallel is napalm. Delivered by long metal tubes that might appear similar to modern flamethrowers, the thick substance could be as dangerous to those using it as those it was aimed at.

Wildfire clung to those it touched and was incredibly flammable. The heat of its fire was only intensified by water, so those jumping into the Thames found no relief. Those running only spread the devastation at terrifying speed. Salisbury laid siege to the Tower as the rest of the army moved north to seek out the king. The citizens quickly located a cache of ordnance of their own and began to return fire against Scales. As the wall began to give way and starvation took hold within the Tower, Scales and Hungerford petitioned Salisbury for peace. Both men received safe conduct out of the city in return for surrendering the Tower and Lord Hungerford was able to slip away. However, when Lord Scales tried to leave the Tower by boat he was attacked and killed, his body thrown into the Thames and washed up later downriver. The capital city would not forgive the man who had wreaked such terror and destruction on his own countrymen.

32. The Battle of Northampton Was the Last of the Wars of the Roses Preceded by Negotiations

The Earl of Warwick's army arrived outside Northampton on the morning of 10 July 1460. He was accompanied by his uncle, Lord Fauconberg, and York's son Edward, Earl of March. It was traditional for potentially prolonged negotiations to take place before any battle with the stated aim of avoiding the spilling of Christian blood. There had been three hours of talks before the First Battle of St Albans and on his arrival, the Earl of Warwick duly sent messages to the king.

An English Chronicle records that Warwick despatched 'certain bishops' to ask the king for an audience for the earl so that he could swear his loyalty to Henry. Humphrey Stafford, Duke of Buckingham, was at the king's side, bearing the scars of Warwick's attack on St Albans, and the duke berated the bishops for daring to appear before their king 'not as bishops to treat for peace, but as men of arms'. The bishops protested that the earl had been forced to bring so many men for his own protection from the true enemies of the king, meaning the court party, which included Buckingham. The duke sent the delegation away, telling them 'The earl of Warwick shall not come to the king's presence, and if he comes he shall die'.

Warwick persisted, next sending a herald of arms to ask the king to provide hostages as a guarantee of Warwick's safety so that he could come before the king. This messenger was also sent away with a flea in his ear. Conflict now became inevitable.

It is always hard to judge the conviction with which either side entered a parley when two armies were lined up against each other. Convention required that certain protocols be observed, even if one or both sides were only going through the motions. The Battle of Northampton that followed Warwick's attempts to gain an audience with the king was the last time during the Wars of the Roses that negotiations took place before a battle, perhaps denoting the dwindling of an archaic tradition, but also marking an escalation in the bitterness of the civil conflict.

33. A Defection Cost the King the Battle of Northampton

When news that Warwick was approaching had reached the royal army, they had set about creating a strong defensible position for themselves. They had thrown up earthworks and planted wooden spikes, positioning guns along the earthworks too. All that work would be undone by a defection from inside the royal camp.

Before the fighting began *An English Chronicle* records that Warwick issued an instruction that 'no man was to lay hands upon the king nor on the common people, but only on lords, knights and squires'. The Burgundian chronicler Waurin also reported that Warwick gave an order not to attack anyone bearing the ragged black staff badge of Lord Grey of Ruthin, 'for it was they who were to give them entry to the park'.

Northampton Battlefield Society continue to research the site and events of the battle with interesting results. It has long been believed that the royal camp had been created in a bend in the River Nene, but it appears more likely now from descriptions of the terrain and the archaeological finds that the site was in a bend in a stream that flowed into the Nene a little further outside the town. It was raining on the day of the battle and that prevented many of the guns from firing, though the oldest cannon ball in England was found beyond the site of the royal camp, suggesting that at least the Yorkist guns were able to fire.

It is believed that Lord Grey had made contact with Warwick as he travelled north and offered to allow him access to the royal camp in the event of a battle. As the two sides moved closer together, Edward, Earl of March, who was commanding the right wing of the Yorkist army in his first battle, was facing Lord Grey's position.

John Whethampstead, abbot of St Albans, recorded that as Edward's men tried to scale the defences, Grey turned his coat and 'the lord with his men met them and, seizing them by the hand, hauled them into the embattled field'.

The royal army was crushed and many were killed or drowned trying to flee across the stream at their back. The fifty-seven-year-old Humphrey, Duke of Buckingham, was among those killed during the fighting, as were Thomas Percy, Lord Egremont, and John Talbot, Earl of Shrewsbury. Warwick, Fauconberg and March took the king to his tent out of the rain and pledged their allegiance to him once again, though he was now firmly in the custody of the Yorkist lords.

34. A Papal Legate Played a Key Role in the Yorkist Victories

Bishop Coppini of Terni was a papal legate, a senior representative of the Pope, who had been sent to England in 1459 to try and encourage Henry VI to support a new crusade against the Turks by Pope Pius II. The bishop also worked as an agent for Francesco Sforza, Duke of Milan, and had been given a secondary mission by the duke, which caused him to be driven out of England.

The king of France, Charles VII, was planning to invade northern Italy and the Duke of Milan hoped to encourage Henry VI to invade France to keep Charles occupied. Bishop Coppini was given short shrift by Margaret for encouraging aggression against her native France and he left for Burgundy nursing his wounded pride. Warwick was possessed of a charming and persuasive personality and managed to convince Coppini that a Yorkist government would be keen to attack France. As a result, the bishop accompanied the Yorkist force when it returned to England and preached their cause, even writing to King Henry to advise him to give the Yorkist lords an audience.

Even the beseeching of a papal representative was not enough to sway Henry or those around him from their suspicion of the Yorkist lords and their aims.

35. The Duke of York Claimed the Throne to Stunned Silence

The date 10 October 1460 is a strong candidate for the real starting of the Wars of the Roses, at least as a dynastic struggle for the crown of England. Following the Yorkist victory at Northampton on 10 July, Richard, Duke of York, took his time before returning to England from his exile in Ireland. When he finally did enter London, he changed the shape of the civil war forever.

What had gone before had, at least by the Yorkist lords, always been characterised as loyal opposition, a struggle to rid the king of evil advisors. York landed in Wales during the second week in September and took his time to travel to London, reuniting with his wife, who had been taken into the custody of her sister, the Duchess of Buckingham, after Ludford Bridge. His journey had the strong sense of a royal progress taken at his leisure.

When he arrived in the capital, York made directly for Westminster where the lords of the land had been gathered in preparation. He marched the length of Westminster Hall, up to the throne that stood empty on the dais and, suddenly hesitating, slowly placed his hand on the cushion on the throne. Abbot Whethamstede wrote that Richard 'walked straight on until he came to the king's throne, upon the covering or cushion laying his hand, in this very act like a man about to take possession of his right, he held it upon it for a short time'. It was a small motion filled with weighty significance. York was claiming the throne of England. He was asserting his right to the crown.

The abbot went on to describe how the duke 'looked eagerly for their applause', expecting to be rapturously welcomed and proclaimed king, only to be met with utter silence. He had horribly misjudged the mood in the room.

It is questionable whether even his closest allies knew what he was going to do, since Warwick remained silent too. Eventually, in the uncomfortable atmosphere, it was left to the Archbishop of Canterbury to approach York and ask whether he wished for an audience with the king. Outraged, and probably embarrassed, the duke bellowed that there was no one in the kingdom who shouldn't rather come to him than he go to them.

York had lost everything and perhaps felt backed into a corner and forced to take such a drastic step. It has long been believed that he had played a long game aimed squarely at the throne. Whatever caused this change of tactic, it altered the nature of the conflict. It was now a straight fight between Henry VI and Richard, Duke of York, for the right to be king of England.

36. An Argument for the Crown Saw the First Recorded Use of the Plantagenet Name

On 16 October 1460, six days after laying a hand on the throne of England, Richard, Duke of York, submitted his detailed claim to the crown to demonstrate that his right was greater than that of Henry VI. In this document the duke is referred to as 'Richard Plantagenet, commonly called duke of York'. This is the first written, recorded account currently in existence of the use of the name Plantagenet to describe the ruling family in England, appearing over 300 years after Henry II had taken the throne as the first of that dynasty in 1154.

The name must have meant something, held some currency in England, otherwise why would Richard use it? Exactly what it meant to those reading and hearing it is unclear, but York traced his lineage back to Henry III to prove his right to wear the crown, so the name Plantagenet must have had royal connotations and been understood to refer to the long-established ruling dynasty in England.

37. THE ACT OF SETTLEMENT WAS DOOMED TO FAIL

When Richard, Duke of York, pressed his claim to the crown of England, it caused outright panic among the establishment. The lords found themselves trapped between a rock and a hard place as crisis threatened and everyone sought to pass the decision on to someone else.

The problems faced by the House of Lords was simple. If they supported the weak Henry and York prevailed, he was unlikely to take kindly as king to those who had denied his right. If they supported York and he failed, then Henry would similarly see them as traitors. The initial response was a request to King Henry to mount his own defence to York's claim, which simultaneously relieved the lords of making a decision and gave Henry the chance to prove he would fight for his crown. Henry, though, had no interest in the fight.

The Lords summoned the king's justices and ordered them to investigate the matter and expose any weakness in York's case. Two days later the justices handed back the hot coal 'because the matter was so high, and touched the king's high estate and regality which was above the law and surpassed their learning'. The king's attorney and his sergeants were called upon next. His reply was simply that 'since the said matter was so high that it surpassed the learning of the justices, it must needs exceed their learning'.

Eventually, the Chancellor, George Neville, instructed the lords present to go away and return with their objections to York's claim, which were to be discussed freely, but each lord was to be required to voice at least one objection. When they came, they were somewhat feeble. The first objection was that they had all sworn oaths of loyalty to Henry, most recently in Parliament in 1459. York batted this aside by insisting that they could not discharge their duty to God to follow the rightful king by any oath to a man. Next, the lords cited the numerous Acts of Parliament confirming the Lancastrian title. York retorted that there had only been one such act in 1406 and that its very existence proved the weakness of the Lancastrian claim. When asked why he had always borne the livery of the House of York rather than that of Lionel of Antwerp, Edward III's second son, descent from whom was the basis of York's claim, the duke replied that it had been to save threatening Henry.

The Act of Settlement eventually passed by Parliament made York and his descendants Henry's legal heir, disinheriting the king's son and the House of Lancaster. It was hardly satisfactory for York, who was ten years older than Henry, particularly if he was as desperate to be king as many have since asserted. Neither was the indomitable Queen Margaret going to sit by and see her beloved son disinherited. The Act of Settlement was only ever going to bring more trouble.

38. Scottish Support Demonstrated
Queen Margaret's Failure to
Understand England

It is possible that Queen Margaret was not far away from the Battle of Northampton. Several sources, including *An English Chronicle*, state that the queen was robbed while fleeing to Wales and some royal possessions were recorded as stolen a few miles from Northampton after the battle. It is believed that Margaret reached the safety of Harlech Castle and was offered protection by her husband's half-brother, Jasper Tudor, Earl of Pembroke. As it became clear that the Yorkist's were developing a stranglehold on power that threatened to disinherit her son, Margaret took ship from Wales to Scotland to look for aid there.

When Margaret arrived, she found a queen in mourning trying to protect her son. James II had been killed on 3 August 1460, a few weeks after the Battle of Northampton in England, by a cannon that exploded. His widow, Mary of Geulders, was trying to ensure and protect the future of her nine-year-old son, who was now James III. Margaret might have seen plenty of similarities in the positions of the two women, but she was determined to get down to business.

By the end of their negotiations, Margaret had what she wanted – an army. The Earl of Angus would lead a strong contingent of Scots soldiers to bolster whatever Lancastrian force Margaret could raise once in England. In return, Margaret had agreed to cede to Scotland the tactically vital border town of Berwick-upon-Tweed, which had changed hands regularly over previous centuries, and offered Scotland a launch pad for future raids into England. Margaret's son Edward was also betrothed to one of Mary's daughters, but the most controversial element of the deal was a result of Margaret's lack of funds. Unable to pay the Scottish soldiers, Margaret instead promised to allow them to take their pay in the form of plunder from English towns that she believed had betrayed her husband.

The deal gave Margaret men that she desperately needed to begin her fightback, but it also showed a reckless lack of understanding of her adopted country. The queen had been in England for fifteen years, half her life, yet was not perturbed by the notion of inviting a Scottish army to invade England and take their pay in what they could steal from the English. With such a long history of border fighting and acrimony, it is not surprising that the English were horrified by the step and frightened of the advance of Margaret's army. Though it perhaps displays Margaret's desperation or her French belief in the Auld Alliance with Scotland, it also showed a lack of understanding of her adopted country and countrymen on Margaret's part that would prove decisive.

39. The Duke of York's Head Was Displayed on Micklegate Bar in York

When news of Margaret's Scottish army reached London, Richard, Duke of York, gathered an army and marched north to intercept them. He arrived at Sandal Castle near Wakefield in December with his seventeen-year-old second son Edmund, Earl of Rutland, his brother-in-law, the Earl of Salisbury, and around 5,000 men. The Duke of Somerset and other Lancastrian lords were making their way to Margaret, swelling her ranks, and York settled in at Sandal to await reinforcements from Wales being mustered by his oldest son Edward, Earl of March.

On 30 December 1460, for reasons that remain unclear, York led his army out of Sandal Castle to face the Lancastrian army before his reinforcements arrived. It has been suggested that his son Edmund had been caught by an ambush while foraging with his men during a Christmas truce. Another suggestion is that Somerset and Northumberland taunted York into marching out by accusing him of cowardice. *An English Chronicle* gives a story corroborated by the Burgundian chronicler Jean de Waurin that may explain why York took the odd step. Salisbury was the senior figure of his branch of the Neville family, but there was another branch led by Ralph Neville, Earl of Westmorland, the son of Salisbury's half-brother. Ralph's younger brother John, Baron Neville, came to York at Sandal and requested a commission to raise men in the duke's name. York gave the authority and Baron Neville returned with 8,000 men at his back. This tipped the numerical advantage over to York and this, *An English Chronicle* asserts, caused him to lead his army out to attack the Lancastrians.

Baron Neville's support had been a trick, probably part of an ongoing feud with Salisbury's branch of the family, and as soon as the Yorkist army left Sandal Castle, Baron Neville turned on them and they were swamped by his 8,000 men and the weight of the Lancastrian army. Edmund, Earl of Rutland, was reportedly captured by Lord Clifford, who exacted revenge for his father's death at St Albans by killing the teenager. Salisbury was captured and imprisoned and later beheaded by an angry mob. Most reports suggest that York was killed in the fighting and his corpse beheaded afterwards, though some say that he was captured and executed afterwards.

The sons of St Albans had their vengeance. The heads of York, Rutland and Salisbury were placed on spikes above Micklegate Bar, one of the main gates into the city of York, with a paper crown stuck to York's head, mocking his royal pretentions. That was to be far from the end, though. The sons of St Albans had won their revenge, but the sons of Wakefield would not take the brutal attack lying down.

40. A Weather Phenomenon Helped Decide the Battle of Mortimer's Cross

Edward, Earl of March, became Duke of York on his father's death and became legal heir to the throne in line with the Act of Settlement. He was still raising men at Ludlow when news of his father's defeat at the Battle of Wakefield arrived. Early in 1461 news also arrived that a Lancastrian army was moving out of Wales behind Jasper Tudor, Earl of Pembroke, his father Owen Tudor and James Butler, Earl of Wiltshire. Edward had to decide whether to hurry to join up with the Earl of Warwick or try and stop the army that had to pass close by his present position. Perhaps the lure of revenge was too great.

The Yorkist army moved a few miles south to Wigmore and was placed in the path of the Lancastrian army. On 2 February the two sides met and although sources for the battle are scarce, several record a weather phenomenon that threatened to undermine the Yorkist unity but was turned to Edward's advantage instead. Several sources place the event on the morning of the battle, though *An English Chronicle* places it the day before.

Around ten o'clock in the morning, three suns reportedly flared in the morning sky. What they witnessed was a parhelion, also known as a sun dog or mock sun. This phenomenon occurs when a cirrus cloud contains ice crystals that fall in a certain pattern. The effect is to create a bright spot to the left, the right or on both sides of the sun, which can have the appearance of two or three suns. In 1461 the superstitious Yorkist soldiers that witnessed the event were afraid that it was a sign of evil that meant they would lose the battle.

Edward took control of the situation, telling his men that the three suns represented the Holy Trinity and meant that God was on their side in the fight to come.

An English Chronicle recorded that he told his men, 'Be of good comfort, and dread not; this is a good sign, for these three suns betoken the Father, the Son, and the Holy Ghost, and therefore let us have a good heart, and in the name of Almighty God go we against our enemies'.

The Yorkist army was convinced by the spin and went on to crush the Lancastrian army in the battle that followed on 2 February 1461. About 3,000–4,000 were reported killed, predominantly from the Welsh Lancastrian force. Jasper Tudor and James Butler escaped into hiding. Edward had snatched a significant victory against the threat of defeat and begun to extract his revenge for Wakefield.

41. An Old Lady Reportedly Cared for Owen Tudor's Decapitated Head

Owen Tudor was around sixty years of age when he fled from the crushing defeat at the Battle of Mortimer's Cross on 2 February 1461. He had lived a long and eventful life, rising from a Welsh gentry family involved in Owain Glyndwr's revolt against Henry IV at the opening of the fifteenth century to marry a queen and father two earls, finally becoming the great-grandfather of the first Tudor king a quarter of a century after his death.

Owen's father, Maredudd ap Tudur, was first cousin to Owain Glyndwr and after the uprising failed, he had moved to London with his son, giving the boy the Anglicised name Owen Tudor. After the death of Henry V in 1422, Owen secured a position in the household of the young widowed queen Catherine of Valois and caught her eye, one story recounting him emerging from swimming in a lake as Catherine passed by and another that while dancing he tripped and fell, his head landing in the queen's lap.

As Catherine fell ill in 1436 in her mid-thirties, she finally revealed her secret marriage to Owen Tudor to her son Henry VI, along with the existence of several children. When Catherine died in 1437, Henry's regency government arrested Owen and threw him into jail. Finally pardoned, Owen must have been delighted that his two sons, his children with Catherine who were not in holy orders, were embraced by Henry and created earls, Edmund as Earl of Richmond and Jasper as Earl of Pembroke. It was meteoric and remarkable rise through society.

Although Owen escaped the Battle of Mortimer's Cross, he was overtaken and captured near Hereford. On the day after the battle, he was brought out into Hereford market square and beheaded, quipping according to *Gregory's Chronicle* 'That head shall lie on the stock that was wont to lie on Queen Katherine's lap'. Gregory goes on to record that a local 'mad woman' cared for the decapitated head after it was placed on the market cross for several days, combing his hair, washing the blood from his face and lighting candles around Owen's head.

42. A Butcher Hanged Himself in the Face of Attacks by Scottish Soldiers

Gregory's Chronicle records an incident that highlights the terror felt by many in England as the Lancastrian army, bolstered by Scottish soldiers promised pay in booty, moved south after their victory at Wakefield.

A butcher from the Dunstable area raised a force of men and took them to the town to confront the approaching Scots, who may have been seeking out the plunder that would make up their pay. Gregory reports that the butcher led his ragtag band of locals onto the field in the king's name to face the Scots only to see around 800 of his men perish in a rout, blamed by Gregory on the 'simple guidance' of the butcher.

The *Londoner's Chronicle* goes on to lament that the butcher, whether for shame at his defeat or because he had lost everything he owned to the marauding Scots, hanged himself shortly after the skirmish. The incident is evidence of the rising fear felt in the south as the hostile army approached the capital and if they were to be successful, Queen Margaret's force would either have to allay those fears or prepare for a fight with the capital city.

43. Andrew Trollope Helped Defeat the Earl of Warwick Despite Being Incapacitated

On 17 February 1461, the Earl of Warwick's Yorkist army intercepted the force led by Queen Margaret that was moving south after the Battle of Wakefield. Many of the Scottish soldiers had abandoned the Lancastrian army by this point, too far from home and too uncertain of pay for their comfort, but Margaret still boasted around 5,000 men, an impressive force during a winter campaign, all wearing the bands of black and crimson with an ostrich feather that was the badge of her son Edward, Prince of Wales.

Andrew Trollope, the leader of the Calais garrison who had left the Yorkist camp at Ludford Bridge, led a lightning strike into the town at the head of a portion of the Lancastrian force. John Neville, Warwick's brother, was still arranging a large section of the Yorkist force outside the town when he found himself caught in a pincer movement between Trollope and the rest of the Lancastrian force. Around 2,500 men were reportedly killed in the early exchange and a contingent of Kentish men deserted Warwick's army, apparently because their leader had been captured at Wakefield but released after giving his oath never to take up arms against the queen or the Prince of Wales again.

Warwick's artillery, which included handguns, a new arrival from the continent, and wildfire seems to have failed either in the damp or in the panic to react. In the shock and confusion, the Yorkist army fled and gave up the field. For his decisive role in the battle, Andrew Trollope was knighted by the seven-year-old Prince of Wales on the instruction of his father King Henry. *Gregory's Chronicle* records that Trollope had trodden on a caltrop, a twisted knot of metal points designed to hamper cavalry charges, during the battle and been left unable to move. When he was knighted, he reportedly protested, probably immodestly, 'I have not deserved it for I slew but fifteen men, for I stood in one place and they came unto me'. The veteran soldier's star was in the ascendancy as the Lancastrian party fought back, but he was to fall very hard soon.

44. The Prince of Wales Ordered the Execution of Two Old Knights

Henry VI was found sitting beneath a tree after the Second Battle of St Albans. He had apparently been oblivious of the battle, laughing and singing as men died in the field. He was discovered being guarded by Lord Bonville and Sir Thomas Kyriell, both men in their late sixties who had declined to flee with their comrades and leave the fragile king without protection. The two men handed the king over to the victorious Lancastrians having been assured by Henry that he would defend them for their protection of him. They were horrified to then be arrested for treason.

King Henry knighted his seven-year-old son after the battle and watched the young Prince of Wales knight several others in turn. The king then stood by as Prince Edward conducted a summary trial of Lord Bonville and Sir Thomas Kyriel for treason. Despite his promise to protect them, King Henry allowed the trial to proceed.

Queen Margaret was reportedly behind the scheme to place her son in charge of the trial. Also present were Henry Holland, Duke of Exeter, and Thomas Courtenay, Earl of Devonshire, who both had property in the West Country near Bonville's. It is likely that the bitter feud between the Courtenay and Bonville families was also a contributory factor in the trial of the two men.

Once found guilty, Margaret reportedly asked her son what form of death the knights should be given, to which the seven-year-old replied that they should have their heads cut off, a sentence that was swiftly delivered. The incident has been used to suggest a cruel and ruthless streak in the young boy, but it seems likely that he was being directed by his mother and those about her who had agendas of their own. Margaret surely wanted to instil more steel in her son than she had found in his father and the lords around her saw an opportunity to score points in an ongoing feud. As the country slipped into civil war, Lancastrian hopes rested not with the feeble, weak-willed Henry but with his son, and Margaret was going to fight with all that she had to protect him and his inheritance. If Edward was to rule and impose order, he was going to need to learn hard lessons and accept his responsibility to dispense firm justice. It was to further this aim in difficult times that the seven-year-old boy was encouraged to act as judge and jury to two old knights who had protected his father.

45. London Closed Its Gates to the King and Queen of England

With the Earl of Warwick defeated and fled westward to meet his cousin Edward, Queen Margaret took her army south, making for London, the capital city of her husband's kingdom. The city had been enthusiastic in its support for Warwick and feared reprisals similar to those at Ludlow, or that the remaining Scots soldiers would be allowed to extract their plunder from the citizens, so they locked their gates against the royal army.

Queen Margaret sent the recently widowed Duchess of Buckingham ahead to London to try and quell the city's fears, but to no avail. The mayor and aldermen wrote to the queen expressing their loyalty but when soldiers led by the Duke of Somerset were seen approaching the walls, a group of citizens attacked them, killing many and driving the rest away.

The mayor and his officials panicked and gathered carts full of money and provisions to send out to the royal army to appease them in the hope of preventing an attack on the city. When the citizens learned of the plan, they seized the keys to the gates and locked them before dividing the contents of the carts up between them.

In a rare act of acquiescence, Margaret turned her army around and marched back to the Lancastrian heartlands in the Midlands. A winter siege of the capital with a dwindling force was in no one's interests. In contrast, Warwick and Edward were welcomed into the city in triumph.

46. The Flower of Craven Were Destroyed at the Battle of Ferrybridge

The Lancastrian army retreated north all the way to York after being barred from London. Edward, Duke of York and Earl of March, attended mass in the capital on 4 March 1461 and was proclaimed king of England, though he refused to undergo a coronation while a Lancastrian army remained in the field. He marched north to meet them in a decisive confrontation.

The Lancastrian army broke the bridge over the River Aire, which crossed the Yorkist path at Ferrybridge. Lord Fitzwalter, leading a Yorkist scouting party, found the ruined crossing and began repairs ahead of the arrival of the main army. The repairs were being watched from cover by a cavalry force under Lord Clifford, who had killed Edward's brother Edmund at Wakefield. They had been sent out from York to find and, if possible, harass the enemy.

The 500-strong cavalry force, known as the Flower of Craven, waited until just before dawn the next morning, 28 March, before riding across the partially repaired bridge and wreaking havoc among the camp while it was still asleep. Lord Fitzwalter was killed and many of his men fled back to the safety of the main army. The Flower of Craven crossed back over the bridge to safety and set a defensible position, guarding the narrow crossing.

Warwick reportedly led a force to attack the crossing, only to find it too well defended and the earl took an arrow to the leg attempting to force a crossing. Even as the rest of the army arrived, no progress could be made. Eventually, Lord Fauconberg, Warwick's uncle, took his cavalry further along the river to the next crossing to flank Clifford. There was skirmishing until dusk, when Clifford saw Fauconberg approaching and ordered the retreat. They rode back towards York with Fauconberg in hot pursuit and Clifford was struck by an arrow to the face after removing his helmet during the ride.

The first blow had been struck in the decisive conflict to come and Edward, putative king of England, had taken his first revenge for his losses at Wakefield, seeing the man who had killed his younger brother dead. The Battle of Ferrybridge was more a skirmish than a real battle, but it is part of the cycle of killings and revenge killings that fuelled the Wars of the Roses and was a prelude to the real decisive action.

47. The Battle of Towton Was the Largest Ever Seen On English Soil

The day 29 March 1461 was Palm Sunday and it was bitterly cold and snowing as the Yorkist and Lancastrian armies woke and prepared for battle near the village of Towton in Yorkshire. Lord Fauconberg, Warwick's uncle and by far the most experienced commander in the field, led the Yorkist army and Henry Beaufort, Duke of Somerset, had command of the royal army in Henry's name, the king remaining in York away from the fighting.

An exchange of arrow fire began the engagement, but Fauconberg had managed to get the wind at his back and position his front line beyond bowshot of the enemy. The Yorkist arrows, with the wind carrying them forward, caused huge numbers of fatalities among the Lancastrians, whose arrows fell short of the Yorkist lines. When the Yorkist archers ran out of arrows, they stepped forward, collected the Lancastrians shafts from the ground and fired them back again.

Somerset ordered his men to advance, with Sir Andrew Trollope leading 7,000 men, including Richard Woodville, Lord Rivers and his son Anthony, who had been given a dressing down in Calais by Salisbury, Warwick and Edward. Henry Percy, Earl of Northumberland, was reportedly meant to charge at the same time but failed to move. The initial charge worked and the Lancastrians chased the Yorkists from the field, believing the battle was won.

The fighting raged on, Polydore Virgil later reporting that it lasted a full ten hours. The advantage swung back and forth with neither side able to make a decisive breakthrough. Finally, John Mowbray, Duke of Norfolk, arrived having become separated from the main Yorkist army during the march and got lost in the snow. The sight of fresh Yorkist reinforcements was enough to finally break the Lancastrian resolve and they began to flee the field, many being slaughtered as they tried to escape.

Estimates place around 100,000 men in the field that day. Several sources number the dead at 29,000. The dead had to be buried in mass grave pits dug into the frozen earth. The Earl of Northumberland was among the dead, completing the vengeance of the sons of Wakefield on the sons of St Albans. Lord Neville and Sir Andrew Trollope were also among the slain.

Gregory's Chronicle lamented that 'many a lady lost her best beloved in the battle' and Waurin coined the phrase 'father did not spare son nor son his father' in relation to this apocalyptic battle. It remains the largest battle fought on English soil in history and took a devastating toll on the population of fighting-age men in England. A decisive victory for the Yorkists, it saw King Henry flee into Scotland and Edward return to London to be crowned Edward IV, the first Yorkist king.

48. Edward IV Ruined a Chance to End the Wars of the Roses

Much of 1462 was spent trying to wrest northern castles from the hands of Lancastrian forces. During the efforts to take Alnwick Castle, Dunstanburgh Castle and Bamburgh Castle, the new Edward IV achieved something of a coup that might have ended the Wars of the Roses once and for all.

Henry Beaufort, Duke of Somerset, was installed at Bamburgh Castle having escaped the field at the Battle of Towton the previous year. The castle was besieged by John Tiptoft, Earl of Worcester, with the assistance of Warwick's brother John Neville, Lord Montagu, and several lords. When Somerset eventually surrendered Bamburgh, he was taken into custody and brought before Edward IV.

During the early part of his reign, Edward tried to conciliate wherever possible, offering any Lancastrian willing to make peace with him an olive branch. When Somerset was brought before him, the two managed to make their peace. Edward agreed to pay Somerset a pension of 1,000 marks to smooth the agreement since the dukedom of Somerset held little income of its own and relied heavily on the Lancastrian crown's favour for money and influence. Edward offered to support the duke to help him come to terms with the new Yorkist government.

Henry Beaufort was the last real military leader within the Lancastrian faction and depriving King Henry's cause of such a prominent figurehead was a real coup that might have brought lasting peace. Somerset had masterminded the victories at Wakefield and St Albans and kept Towton a close-run affair before ultimately losing the day. Henry and Margaret's cause would have been seriously weakened, perhaps delivered a fatal blow, by the loss of Somerset.

Six months after the agreement was made, Somerset fled north across the border to Scotland and back to King Henry's side. His pension had gone unpaid, leaving him impoverished, and he had not found a place in the halls of power under the new regime. He decided that his future lay with the Lancastrian cause once more and Edward lost a chance to bring peace a lot closer by bringing Somerset into the fold.

49. Elizabeth Woodville Was Not Really a Commoner of No Standing

In September 1464, Edward IV dropped a bombshell during a council meeting that would shape the remainder of his kingship and beyond. Edward announced to a stunned room that he had married in secret a few months earlier, around 4 May. The new queen consort was Elizabeth Woodville, a woman who has long been deemed a commoner unsuitable for a king. She was a widow, her first husband Sir John Grey having been killed fighting for the Lancastrian army at the Second Battle of St Albans leaving her with two sons, Thomas and Richard. However, she was not exactly low born.

Elizabeth Woodville was the oldest of thirteen children who lived to adulthood born to Richard Woodville, Lord Rivers, and his wife, Jacquetta of Luxembourg. Richard had been a soldier in France and was the son of Sir Richard Woodville, a chamberlain to John, Duke of Bedford, Henry VI's uncle. After Bedford's death in 1435, Richard secretly married the widowed duchess in a match that caused a scandal but won him a barony.

Jacquetta of Luxembourg was far from low born. Her father was Peter of Luxembourg, Count of Saint-Pol, Conversano and Brienne, who was a descendant of John, Duke of Brittany, and his wife Beatrice of England, a daughter of Henry III. Her mother was Margaret of Baux, daughter of Francesco del Balzo, 1st Duke of Andria, and she could trace her ancestry back to Simon de Montfort, Earl of Leicester, and Eleanor of England, a daughter of King John and sister to Henry III. Jacquetta's older brother Louis of Luxembourg was Count of Saint-Pol, de Brienne, de Ligny, and Conversano and was Constable of France. Jacquetta was also an English duchess after her marriage to John, Duke of Bedford.

The Earl of Warwick had been championing a French marriage for Edward to solidify links with that nation and had returned from France with a marriage agreement ready to be sealed by the king when Edward announced that he was already married and intended to favour a Burgundian alliance. Richard Woodville was elevated to the peerage as Earl Rivers and Elizabeth's family attracted disdain as her siblings snapped up prize marriages and appointments, one nineteen-year-old brother marrying the dowager Duchess of Norfolk who was sixty-five, a sister marrying the Duke of Buckingham, another marrying Viscount Bourchier and then the heir of the Earl of Kent. Elizabeth's oldest son from her first marriage became Marquis of Dorset and is an ancestor of Henry Grey, Duke of Suffolk, father to Lady Jane Grey, the nine-day queen. Her family undoubtedly benefitted from her illustrious marriage, as might be expected, but she was not quite the commoner history has remembered her as.

50. Two Small Battles Interrupted Almost a Decade of Peace

As part of his political manoeuvres King Edward was close to securing peace with France, Burgundy and Scotland in early 1464. If successful, he would manage to starve the remaining Lancastrian resistance of support and further secure his position. John Neville, Lord Montagu, brother of the Earl of Warwick, was despatched with 5,000 men north to escort a Scottish embassy to meet the king but he was attacked on his way and on the journey back.

The Lancastrians panicked at the threat posed to their position and the Duke of Somerset, accompanied by Lords Roos and Hungerford and several thousand men, marched south into England to intercept Lord Montagu. The two armies faced each other at Hedgeley Moor in Northumberland on 25 April 1464. After initial archery exchanges, Montagu advanced only to see the Lancastrian wings under Lords Roos and Hungerford crumble and flee. Somerset was forced to retreat and his forces were scattered.

Lord Montagu continued north to collect the Scottish ambassadors, only to find himself presented with the same army blocking his path south at Hexham on 15 May 1464. The Lancastrians had barely finished arranging themselves when they were under attack. Lord Roos ran almost immediately again. Lord Hungerford was killed and Somerset and Roos were captured and executed in Hexham.

The battles of Hedgeley Moor and Hexham did not pose much of a threat to Edward in the end, but did deprive Henry of his staunchest supporter in the Duke of Somerset. Henry himself had moved west and spent some time at Muncaster Castle, leaving his host Sir John Pennington a glass bowl in thanks and blessing him with a promise that as long as it remained intact the family would always have male heirs. The bowl is still at Muncaster Castle today and since the gift there has been a male Pennington to inherit it.

Henry moved next to Bolton Hall where he was given shelter by the Pudsay family before moving on to Waddington Hall. Word of Henry's whereabouts became known and men led by Sir James Harrington stormed into the hall after almost a year of safety for the old king. Henry reportedly escaped the Hall and tried to flee across the River Ribble only to be caught in Clitheroe Woods. He was taken to London with his ankles bound to his stirrups and handed over to Edward IV. Henry was placed into the Tower of London and Sir James Harrington was rewarded with a hundred marks for his service.

51. ANTHONY WOODVILLE TOOK PART IN THE MOST FAMOUS TOURNAMENT OF THE AGE

When a group of women of Edward IV's court crowded around Anthony Woodville, Lord Scales, at Sheen Palace on Wednesday 17 April 1465 and fixed a gold collar to his thigh, he knew all too well what was happening. He was being challenged to meet Anthony, the Bastard of Burgundy, illegitimate son of the Duke of Burgundy, in a tournament that would be remembered as one of the events of the century.

The tournament finally took place in the summer of 1467, the Bastard of Burgundy arriving at Gravesend in late May. He was given a state welcome before being presented to King Edward. The tournament was opened amid great pageantry on 10 June and on the following day the crowd were treated to the main event: a one-on-one duel between Anthony Woodville, the English champion, and the Bastard of Burgundy, the finest soldier in his land. The two men fought in shining polished armour, each wielding a war axe and carrying a dagger sheathed at their waist. Lauded as a classic contest that would be famous for all history, King Edward eventually had to declare the match a draw and have the men parted before either came to real harm. Anthony Woodville's armour was reported to bear several slices made by the pointed back end of the Bastard's axe.

Over the following three days there were several sets of contests between the English knights and their Burgundians counterparts. The English appeared to have the upper hand when the event was abruptly brought to a close by news of the death of the Bastard's father Philip, Duke of Burgundy. Philip's legitimate son and heir Charles had sent an offer to King Edward to marry his sister Margaret of York and King Edward was minded to agree, though the Earl of Warwick bitterly opposed the match. The Bastard of Burgundy returned home to aid his half-brother and mourn their father and Edward agreed to the marriage of his sister to Duke Charles.

The politically well-informed writer of the *Crowland Chronicle* insisted that Warwick's subsequent feud with Edward was not, as many believed, the result of the king's marriage to Elizabeth Woodville when the earl had negotiated a match with a French princess, writing instead that it was a result of Edward's Burgundian alliances and Warwick's personal hatred of Charles, the new duke, claiming that Warwick 'pursued that man with a most deadly hatred'.

The tournament ended on a flat note due the circumstances. Anthony Woodville was entering the ranks of legendary tournament knights but the closer Edward moved to Burgundy, the more he alienated his most powerful subject, the Earl of Warwick.

52. Warwick Had His Daughter Married to the King's Brother Against Edward's Will

Richard Neville, Earl of Warwick, was at the very pinnacle of his family's powers at the beginning of the 1460's when he helped Edward IV become the first Yorkist king. As the decade went on, the rich and powerful earl saw his relationship with his cousin the king slip until the two were almost estranged. The queen's Woodville family were supplanting the earl and his influence over the king dwindled until he was willing to take no more.

Warwick had no sons to leave his vast estates to, but he had two daughters. The Woodville women had been cornering the marriage market but the earl had been trying for some time to see his eldest daughter Isabel married to King Edward's brother George, Duke of Clarence. George was next in line to the throne until Edward had sons and the match would bring Warwick closer to the centre of power once again but Edward had blocked the match at every turn.

The king had blocked the marriage on grounds of consanguinity because George and Isabel were first cousins once removed, though that may have simply been a convenient excuse to continue the policy of excluding Warwick. As matters reached a crisis point in 1469, Warwick applied for papal dispensation to allow the marriage despite the relationship behind Edward's back, his wealth and influence abroad allowing him to secure the permission he needed.

As soon as the dispensation arrived from Rome, Warwick took a ship to Calais, taking with him Isabel and George, Duke of Clarence. The couple were married on 11 July 1469 in Calais in defiance of the king's restriction. Warwick had succeeded in bringing the king's brother to his side, the lure of a vast inheritance perhaps helping to tempt George to act behind his brother's back. From Calais, Warwick issued letters accompanied by Robin of Redesdale's manifesto, which berated the influence enjoyed by the Woodvilles and others Warwick clearly considered beneath him. Warwick was now in a similar position to Edward's father, Richard, Duke of York, feeling that he offered loyal opposition. He had the heir to the throne in his camp and it seemed that a repeat of history was on the cards.

53. Edward Sealed Neville Opposition by Dispossessing John Neville

John Neville had been a loyal servant to Edward IV. As Lord Montagu, he had provided vital military support in the effort to place Edward on the throne. John's reward for this loyalty had been the grant of the former Percy earldom of Northumberland, seized from the Neville family's enemy after the Battle of Towton in 1461 and given to John in 1464, solidifying the Neville grip on the north of England. John had reportedly taken decisive action against the uprising led by Robin of Holderness in favour of the Percy cause. Although he appears to have taken no part in the revolt against Edward led by his brothers the Earl of Warwick and George, Archbishop of York, he was about to be punished by Edward in spectacular fashion.

George Neville had been replaced as Chancellor in 1467 after refusing to attend the tournament involving Anthony Woodville and the Bastard of Burgundy as part of Warwick's campaign against an allegiance with Burgundy. John had remained solidly loyal to Edward, but the king suddenly decided that he wished to rehabilitate Henry Percy, the heir to the Earl of Northumberland killed at Towton. Henry Percy had been petitioning the king regularly for the return of the Percy inheritance and, possibly as a foil to Neville power in the region, Edward finally agreed to his request. The main problem was that John Neville currently held the title and lands Henry Percy wanted.

In 1470, Edward deprived John Neville of the earldom of Northumberland and returned it to Henry Percy. To compensate John, he was created Marquis Montagu, the rank of marquis sitting above that of an earl but below a duke. In theory, it was a promotion for John but in reality he lost all of the regional and national wealth and influence that went with the Northumberland titles. John himself complained that the grant was 'a magpie's nest', meaning that it was an empty title and offered no income to support him. John's son George was created Duke of Bedford and promised a marriage to Edward's oldest daughter Elizabeth. It seems unlikely that Edward ever really intended to give his first, and at this time only, child to George Neville and perhaps John knew as much.

John Neville surely felt hard done to and ill-rewarded for his loyalty to Edward. For his part, the king seems to have been stepping up his efforts to dislodge the chokehold the Nevilles had on northern politics and which Warwick felt he should possess on the national stage. Restoring the Percy family offered a natural and potent foil to Neville influence. It also made it clear to the Neville family, including John, that their time in power was rapidly coming to an end.

54. Robin Hood Inspired Northern Uprisings That Marked a New Beginning of Trouble in England

The spring of 1469 saw the rupturing of the peace in England, which had been growing more fragile. King Edward and the Earl of Warwick were increasingly at odds in a repeat of the problems between Henry VI and Richard, Duke of York. The Woodville family of Edward's queen were increasingly at the centre of the court and exerting influence over the king, which made Warwick feel pushed aside, a situation he was not willing to tolerate indefinitely.

Sources for the uprisings that broke out in the north are scarce and often contradictory, perhaps betraying the southern focus of political life. Some sources point to three revolts, others to two, with leadership and motives confused. There is a suggestion that there was an abortive uprising either in late March or early May in the name of a Robin of Redesdale, but more certain is a serious gathering of rebels under the leadership of a man known as Robin of Holderness.

Stories of Robin Hood were widespread and popular by this period. The earliest text of a written ballad of Robin Hood is *Robin Hood and the Monk*, written down in the late fifteenth century. Robin Hood also makes an appearance in the late fourteenth-century masterpiece *Piers Plowman* and it is likely that the story had an oral history dating back even further. The name Robin was used in these uprisings to disguise the true identity of the leader but also to identify the revolt with positive aims for the interest of the kingdom and the common man against a corrupt crown.

The uprising under Robin of Holderness seems to have been aimed at promoting Percy family interests against the strength of the Neville family in the region. In early July there was a revolt led by Robin of Redesdale, which had links to the Neville affinity. The identity of this 'Robin' remains unclear but it has been suggested that it was Sir John Conyers, a retainer of the Earl of Warwick. John Neville, who had been given the Percy earldom of Northumberland, made no effort to oppose the uprising and Neville men were found among those involved in the rising.

King Edward was in East Anglia when he received news of the uprising. Gathering a force and marching north, reports soon reached Edward that the revolt was more serious than first thought with as many as 20,000 men suggested to be following Robin of Redesdale. Outnumbered, King Edward retired to Nottingham Castle and called for reinforcements. He had underestimated Warwick's disaffection.

55. The Earl of Warwick Took Edward IV Prisoner

The rebels had won a great victory at the Battle of Edgecote Moor, but there was another coup when George Neville, Archbishop of York and younger brother of the Earl of Warwick, learned that King Edward had been abandoned by his army at Nottingham. In a village just outside Coventry, the archbishop took the king of England into his custody and delivered him to Warwick Castle and the custody of his brother, the earl.

Warwick claimed that he had taken the king into protective custody because men of the south were plotting to murder him. It was for this reason too, the earl claimed, that he moved Edward north to his fortress at Middleham in Yorkshire. With the king under his control, Warwick began to govern in his cousin's name, much as Richard, Duke of York, had done when Henry VI had been king. However, Warwick found it harder than he had imagined. Edward was neither a feeble character nor incapacitated by illness and Warwick had launched a direct attack on Edward's government by executing men like Richard Woodville and the earls of Pembroke and Devon. Men refused to obey Warwick, uncertain whether the instructions he gave really came from Edward or not.

Government still relied entirely on the person of the king. In 1454 and 1455, Richard, Duke of York, had operated with the benefit of an Act of Parliament to give him authority. Warwick had no such token of his position and was not seeking to be conciliar in his style. Warwick found it increasingly hard to operate the country with the king a prisoner. The real problem came when a Lancastrian force led by Sir Humphrey Neville used the disruption in England to launch a raid over the border from Scotland. Warwick found himself unable to raise a force to repel the incursion.

Warwick was left with no choice. He ordered Edward's release and the king appeared in York on 10 September, a warm welcome guaranteeing that he could swiftly raise the men needed to fend off the Lancastrian attack. After making a magnificent return to London, Edward summoned a Great Council at Westminster where great show was made of a reconciliation between the two sides. The Crowland chronicler was under no illusion that Edward had no intention of forgiving Warwick, writing that 'there probably remained, on the one side, deeply seated in his mind, the injuries he had received and the contempt which had been shown to majesty'. Edward would not let the insult lie.

56. A Squabble Over Billeting Helped Lose the Battle of Edgecote Moor

William Herbert, Earl of Pembroke, and Humphrey Stafford, Earl of Devon, were bringing reinforcements to Edward IV at Nottingham Castle to help fight Robin of Redesdale's rebellion. The two forces converged on 25 July 1469 near Banbury to make the rest of the march north together, but a problem with finding lodgings for both armies led to trouble the following morning.

Warkworth's Chronicle reported that William Herbert brought with him a huge force of 43,000 Welshmen while Devon added 7,000 archers to the force. Warkworth then goes on to report that the lords 'fell into variance for their lodging' as a result of which Pembroke, who appears to have prevailed in the argument, secured billeting in Banbury and Devon was forced to find room for him and his men several miles away.

In the early morning of the next day, 26 July 1469, Robin of Redesdale's northern force fell upon Pembroke's men outside Banbury having marched passed the king at Nottingham to meet up with Warwick's force crossing from Calais. The prospect of catching the large force of Welshmen spread across their path unawares was too tempting for the northerners, though the willingness of 20,000 to attack 43,000 suggests that Warkworth's figure for Pembroke's force might have been incorrect.

In the absence of archers the battle moved directly to intense hand-to-hand fighting, which was evenly balanced for the morning. Around 1 o'clock, Pembroke received news that Devon was finally approaching to reinforce him but at the same time Warwick's banners came into view. Fearing that the large force at his back was made up of professional soldiers, which it was not, Pembroke's men were routed. The fight was remembered as the Battle of Edgecote Moor and marked a renewal of violence.

Pembroke and his brother Sir Richard Herbert were captured and executed the next day on Warwick's orders. A few days later, Warwick caught up with the Earl of Devon and had him executed too. On 12 August the earl ordered the execution after a swift show trial of Richard Woodville, Earl Rivers, the king's father-in-law and Richard's second son John Woodville. A fresh round of feuding and reprisals were threatening to destroy the peace Edward had spent a decade building.

57. Sir Robert Welles Watched His Father Executed Before the Battle of Losecote Field

During February 1470, King Edward's Master of the Horse was attacked at his manor in Lincolnshire by his neighbour Lord Welles. Richard, Lord Welles, rode with his son Sir Robert and their associate Sir Thomas Dymoke to Sir Thomas de Burgh's manor, drove him out, tore down the house and stole cattle and any other property they could lay their hands on.

Edward could not have been unaware that not only was Lord Welles a second cousin of the Earl of Warwick, but that his stepmother was the widow of John Beaufort, Duke of Somerset, giving him strong links to both Warwick and the hibernating Lancastrian cause. Edward immediately summoned Lord Welles, refusing to accept a plea of ill-health and offering Lord Welles a safe conduct. The chastened baron was forced to apologise and make his peace with the king.

Sir Robert Welles had been gathering a force of men in his father's absence. He would later claim that his father had instructed him to be ready to fall upon the capital if Edward mistreated him, but news of the muster reached the king and he raised his own army to march north and meet the threat. Edward ordered Sir Robert to disband but he refused. Lord Welles was forced to write to his son instructing him to surrender to the king but still Sir Robert refused.

On 12 March 1470, Edward's army lined up opposite the rebel force led by Sir Robert. The king had Lord Welles brought out before the army and summarily executed in front of his son. With that, Edward's army attacked and the poorly disciplined rebel force immediately fled. The Battle of Losecote Field took its name from the fact that so many fleeing men threw off their jackets, either to disguise their allegiance or to lighten their load to speed their escape.

Sir Robert Welles and Sir Thomas Dymoke were captured. Robert was interrogated and claimed that Edward's brother George, Duke of Clarence, had sent his men to incite them to rebel and that the Earl of Warwick had sent one of his men with a ring as a token of the earl's part in the planned uprising. Robert claimed in his confession that he had been told that the purpose of the revolt was 'to make the Duke of Clarence king'. Robert and Dymoke were executed, though the *Crowland Chronicle* notes that the king 'showed grace and favour to the ignorant and guiltless multitude', excusing the soldiers and punishing only their leaders.

If Edward harboured any doubts about the intentions of Warwick and Clarence, the Welles Uprising dispelled them and made it clear that he was facing a serious threat.

58. John Tiptoft Earned the Nickname the Butcher of England for His Cruelty

During the skirmishing between Warwick and Anthony Woodville's men on the south coast as Warwick tried to flee England, several men were captured from Warwick's force and they felt the full weight of the firm hand of Edward IV's justice.

Edward's Constable was a man named John Tiptoft, Earl of Worcester. In his twenties, during the 1450s, Tiptoft had served as Lord High Treasurer and Lord Deputy of Ireland. Tiptoft was out of the country when the troubles between the houses of Lancaster and York intensified, travelling on a pilgrimage to the Holy Land and spending two years at the University of Padua on his way back where he developed an impressive reputation as a Latin scholar.

Tiptoft returned to England in 1461, after Edward IV had become king. Untainted by having had to take sides in the battles of the previous months, Tiptoft was welcomed by Edward and entered the new king's service with a glowing past and promising future. In 1467, Tiptoft was appointed Lord Deputy of Ireland again, replacing Thomas Fiztgerald, Earl of Desmond, who was then prosecuted for treason and executed. Some sources claim that Tiptoft was the architect of Desmond's fall and some claim he also ordered the deaths of Desmond's two young sons while they were at school.

As Constable of England, Tiptoft was back in England as trouble broke out. The Constable was essentially responsible for law, order and justice in the country and presided over a martial court, which gave him the right to try and decide cases of treason based on evidence that he had seen. The accused had no right of appeal and the sentence was usually death. The Constable's court operated outside the usual rules of justice, denying the accused a fair trial, but was designed to deliver swift and firm justice in times of military necessity.

Tiptoft delivered harsh justice on the men taken during Warwick's flight. *Warkworth's Chronicle* records that twenty gentlemen and yeomen were convicted of treason and given a gruesome execution, no doubt meant to act as a lesson to others. All twenty were hanged, drawn and quartered, the traditional punishment for a traitor, but it did not end there. Tiptoft ordered the beheaded corpses to be strung up by their feet and wooden spikes, sharpened at each end, driven from the buttocks through the body and into the ground. The heads were then placed on top of the spikes in a gruesome spectacle more at home in Vlad the Impaler's Wallachia than Yorkist England.

John Tiptoft's reputation was ruined and soon he was captured by Lancastrian forces and executed. His cruelty earned him the nickname 'the Butcher of England', though it is unlikely he acted without Edward's authority, if not approval. Certainly, the king did not censure the Constable for his extreme actions.

59. The Earl of Warwick Lost His First Grandchild at Sea

After the Battle of Losecote Field, Warwick and Clarence, who had been heading north to Lancashire in search of support, perhaps from Lord Stanley and his large retinue, abruptly turned south and tried to flee back to the safety of Calais. Edward pushed westward to try and intercept them and sent a flurry of orders out to try and cut off their escape.

Warwick made first for his flagship *The Trinity* on the south coast, only to find that Anthony Woodville, now Earl Rivers after his father's execution at Warwick's hands, had arrived before him and seized his ships. After a brief skirmish, Warwick and Clarence made their escape and managed to hire a boat further along the coast that would take them to Calais.

Orders were also sent by the king to Lord Wenlock, Warwick's deputy in Calais, instructing him to deny entry to the fortress to the earl and duke. Despite being a long-term ally of the earl, Lord Wenlock chose to obey the king's instruction and had the town sealed. When Warwick's boat appeared before Calais, Wenlock refused to allow him into the harbour. Forced further along the coast, they were also denied refuge in the lands of Edward's ally, and Warwick's old foe, Charles, Duke of Burgundy.

Eventually, Warwick's boat was forced to make land in France and the earl and his son-in-law the duke fell into the ready, scheming hands of Louis XI, king of France, known as the Universal Spider for his diplomatic web-weaving. The family were too late to prevent tragedy striking, though. Warwick's oldest daughter Isabel, Clarence's wife, was on board ship with them and was heavily pregnant. She went into labour on the rough seas outside Calais and with aid denied to them, she gave birth in the unsuitable surroundings of the hired boat. The little girl, named Anne, did not survive long enough to reach dry land.

Warwick had lost his first grandchild. George and Isabel had lost their first child. It was a cruel price to pay for their action against the king and the three can only have blamed one man for their loss and the distress it caused. Edward had denied them the help that might have saved George and Isabel's baby. The bitter political wrangling took on a new and terrible personal edge.

60. Louis XI of France Engineered a Powerful Alliance Against Edward IV

When the Earl of Warwick and Duke of Clarence made their forced landing in France, Louis XI began weaving his webs of intrigue with renewed vigour. Henry VI's wife Margaret of Anjou, now forty years old, was in France with her son, the seventeen-year-old Edward of Westminster at the time Warwick arrived. King Louis saw an opportunity to destabilise Edward's government and was keen to do so since Edward had allied himself with Louis's enemies in Burgundy. The problem was how to bring together the bitter former queen and the man who had played a leading role in dislodging her and her husband.

Louis went to work on Warwick, convincing him that Margaret and her son represented his best hope of a return to power. If King Henry was put back on the throne, he would be easy for Warwick to control. Margaret, who had been living at Louis' expense, was brought to court and persuaded that Warwick also represented her best hope of regaining her son's inheritance. Louis succeeded in convincing both sides that they had to put their differences aside and Margaret agreed to give Warwick an audience. When the earl entered and knelt before the former queen, Margaret reportedly did not permit him to rise from the uncomfortable position for quarter of an hour.

Finally, an agreement was reached that Warwick's younger daughter Anne would marry Margaret's son Edward of Westminster to cement the alliance between them. Warwick would have the opportunity to rule in King Henry's name and to see a grandchild on the throne of England. Margaret would have the chance to win back her son's inheritance, no doubt hoping that she could cut short Warwick's influence as her son became a more important figure.

Critically, the scheme required that Warwick abandon his original plans to place George, Duke of Clarence, on the throne. George had abandoned his own brother because of Warwick's promise to make him king and now his father-in-law was replacing him at the head of the plan with the arch enemy of his house. George had little to gain from the restoration of the House of Lancaster and his only consolation was that he might still become king if Henry and Prince Edward died without issue. It was a relegation of his position that the young duke was unlikely to accept with good grace. While stuck in France with his father-in-law, he was left with little alternative but to go along with the plan. If reports by the Burgundian chronicler Philippe de Commynes were correct, though, one of the Duchess of Clarence's ladies slipped through Calais with a message from King Edward offering an olive branch to George. Edward was already sowing seeds of disunity among the new alliance and George had a way out of the situation he had got himself into.

61. THE NEVILLE FAMILY DROVE EDWARD IV OUT OF ENGLAND

In August 1470, Warwick landed at Plymouth with a fleet supplied by Louis XI. As he marched to London, men flocked to the popular earl's cause. King Edward was at Lynn in Norfolk when news reached him of the landing. He gathered around 3,000 men quickly, aided by his friend Lord Hastings and his brother-in-law Anthony Woodville, Earl Rivers. He asked Charles the Bold to be ready to send a fleet against Warwick's and sent a further commission north to Marquis Montagu to raise 6,000 more men.

John Neville, Marquis Montagu, was Warwick's younger brother. He had remained apparently loyal to Edward and taken no part in his brother's attacks on the king. Edward seemed confident that John was still on side and began preparations to repel Warwick, according to Commynes taking up residence at a moated manor that could be easily defended. As Warwick marched north, John marched south with his large force. It was now that the problems Edward has stored up in his policy returned to bite him. John Neville had been Earl of Northumberland for five years before Edward decided to return that title to the Neville family's arch enemies, the Percy family. Although he had, on paper, further elevated John as Marquis, John had found himself impoverished and unable to support himself in a title that had no associated income. John's son had been made a duke and promised a match to Edward's daughter Elizabeth, but with the king's policy of pushing the Neville family away from the centre of power it is possible that John doubted this was ever going to be realised.

Warkworth reported that as John's men came within a few miles of Lynn they began to call King Henry's name, causing King Edward to panic. Whether this was a lack of discipline on the part of John's men or an early warning to a king John was still not willing to openly attack. The chants exposed Edward's vulnerability and he realised he was caught in a trap that was about to snap shut about him as Warwick approached from the south and John Neville from the north.

Realising that he had little choice, Edward sent his men away with a promise that he would return and hired a ship to take him to Burgundy. The king left his country on 2 October 1470 with Lord Hastings and Earl Rivers. Also on board was the king's youngest brother Richard, Duke of Gloucester. Despite the revolt by his other brother, George, and Warwick, the man in whose household Richard had been raised, the young duke remained loyal to his oldest brother the king. The day that they took ship to flee England into an uncertain exile was Richard's eighteenth birthday and the second time Richard had been forced out of the country by the Wars of the Roses, having been sent to Burgundy with George after their father's death in 1460.

62. A Word Had to Be Invented to Describe Henry VI's Return to the Throne

With Edward IV driven out of England, Warwick was quick to release Henry VI from the Tower of London, give him a royal makeover and present him to the people as their rightful king, previously wrongfully dispossessed but now restored. Warwick's own part in that dispossession was glossed over. This was to be the first time a king who had been removed from the throne would be put back upon it. There was no precedent and no one even had a name to describe what was happening.

Henry was led to the Palace of Westminster where he was ceremonially re-crowned. A Parliament was summoned in King Henry's name and opened with the message 'Revertimini ad me filii revertentes', 'Return to me oh ye rebelling children'. Henry was being presented by Warwick as the comfortable father figure of the nation, offering stability and certainty. The old king was extending an olive branch to those who had betrayed him and giving them the opportunity to return to their allegiance.

The problem was that people didn't necessarily want a return to the problems Henry VI had overseen. Warkworth believed that Edward had failed to deliver on his promises of a new start and a bright future, but Henry had been king during the darkest times. The return to the comfort of Henry's rule and the Lancastrian dynasty needed to be marked as a new beginning too. Henry began signing official documents 'Anno regni Regis Henrici Sexti quadragesimo nono, et readempcionis sue regie potestatis primo', 'Forty-ninth year of the reign of King Henry VI, and the first since his royal readeption'.

This novel circumstance was given an entirely made-up name – a readeption. The word seems to have been created in an attempt to describe a situation in which a previously deposed king is returned to the throne. Warwick's deft management of spin and publicity can be seen in the signature used by Henry. The readeption was marked as the forty-ninth year of Henry's rule, giving the impression of continuity and stability, but also as 'the first since his royal readeption', giving it the added sheen of something new and promising.

Warwick was the master of propaganda but he needed to demonstrate now that he could govern. There were plenty of problems though. The Lancastrians, overjoyed at the return of Henry, were naturally suspicious of Warwick, their enemy for so long and an architect of their downfall. Money was in short supply and Warwick was being forced to spend his own vast wealth propping up Henry's government, a situation he could not sustain indefinitely. Margaret and her son, the real strength of the Lancastrian cause, were still in France waiting for a signal of safety before they would return, making Henry's supporters more nervous. It was not going to be easy.

63. The Battle of Nibley Green Was the Last Between Private Armies in English History

After years of peace, the tension that was erupting into conflict between King Edward and his most powerful subject Richard Neville, Earl of Warwick, was destabilising the country and bringing out bad habits as local feuds were once more settled outside of the courts.

On 20 March 1470, the Battle of Nibley Green took place in Gloucestershire as part of the lawlessness. Lord Berkley of Berkeley Castle and Lord Lisle of Wooten had been locked in a dispute over the Berkley inheritance, which Lord Lisle made a claim on through his mother, the Countess of Shrewsbury. As law and order broke down, the men resolved to settle the matter by battle, bringing less than a thousand men each to the village of Nibley Green. Lord Berkley won the fight that followed and Lord Lisle was killed. Lord Berkley went on to ransack Lisle's manner at Wotton-under-Edge and later ordered the south aisle of St Martin's Church in Nibley Green to be built to celebrate his victory and commemorate those who died in the battle, many of who were buried in the churchyard there.

The Battle of Nibley Green was the last battle on English soil between two entirely private armies fought to settle a personal dispute. It was also a symptom of trouble to come as the Yorkist grip on power slipped.

64. Edward IV's First Son Was Born in Sanctuary at Westminster Abbey

Queen Elizabeth Woodville had laid down provisions to hold the Tower of London against Warwick as he swept north but when news of her husband's flight reached her she had a tough decision to make. Elizabeth was heavily pregnant and unable to make a perilous and uncertain journey to the continent. Instead, she chose to move into sanctuary at Westminster Abbey.

King Henry's Parliament reversed the legitimacy of Edward IV's kingship and overturned the attainders against Lancastrian lords. Edmund Beaufort, younger brother of Henry, was finally able to become 4th Duke of Somerset. Henry Holland, Duke of Exeter, who had been forced to divorce Edward's sister Anne, was restored as was Henry's half-brother Jasper Tudor, who retook his earldom of Pembroke, and John de Vere, Earl of Oxford. Early in 1471 these men found the confidence to begin to return to England and try to re-establish the authority they had lost a decade earlier.

On 2 November 1470, Queen Elizabeth gave birth to a son, the first son born to Edward IV. The boy was named for his absent father and although he was the son Edward had waited for, his future must have seemed incredibly uncertain. Elizabeth must have feared for the future of her new son and the couple's three daughters as Lancastrians set about restoring their power around her sanctuary.

65. Edward IV Tried To Return to England as Duke of York

On 2 March 1471, Edward IV set sail from Flanders with a small group of his supporters intending to take back his crown. Queen Margaret and her seventeen-year-old son Prince Edward took to their ships from France on 14 March but storms delayed their departure until 14 April. King Edward's ships were buffeted by the same storms and he was unable to land in Norfolk after finding the Earl of Oxford's brother defending the coast. Travelling on north, his ships were scattered and he finally managed to reach the shore at Ravenspur in Yorkshire, the exact same spot on which Henry IV had landed when he came to claim Richard II's crown.

Edward's men were spread out along the Yorkshire coast and it took some time for them to reassemble. An unknown member of Edward's party recorded the journey back into England and although *The Arrival of King Edward IV* is obvious in its bias, it nevertheless provides an invaluable insight into the path back to the throne.

According to *The Arrival*, Edward did not receive the rapturous welcome he had hoped for. Despite the title his family had held, Yorkshire was not the centre of his family's power. Here, Warwick and the Percy family held sway and sympathies were more Lancastrian than Yorkist. The writer notes that there was lingering affection in the region for Edward's father Richard, Duke of York, and some called for Edward to be given back the dukedom rather than seeking the crown. Henry IV had made a similar plea to only want his Lancastrian ducal inheritance when he landed at Ravenspur in 1399 and it gave Edward an idea.

As he approached the city of York, Edward and his followers maintained their insistence that Edward only wanted to be recognised as Duke of York. All around them were reports of large forces of men mustered against them but none seemed willing to confront the 6-foot-4 king, who had never lost a battle. York was convinced to open its gates to Edward in the first victory of his return. As Edward set off south, he passed by John Neville, Marquis Montagu's force unmolested and met no resistance from Henry Percy, Earl of Northumberland. While they didn't support him, their inaction was a positive signal to Edward.

When he reached Nottingham and more friendly country, Edward began to find men finally flocking to his cause. Learning that Lancastrian forces were gathering around him and that Warwick was in Coventry, Edward marched to the town and challenged the earl to come out and face him. When the two could not agree terms between them, Edward marched on and towards two decisive battles.

66. King Edward Reportedly Witnessed a Miracle at Daventry

George, Duke of Clarence, was convinced to return to his allegiance to his brother Edward IV, who had been courting him while still in France and had continued to tempt him since his return to England. Their youngest brother Richard, Duke of Gloucester, reportedly acted as the go-between to help secure the return of Clarence, whose position had radically changed since he had been promised the crown by Warwick. Clarence brought with him around 4,000 men, a significant blow to Warwick and boost to Edward's cause.

The royal brothers continued southward, making for London. On Palm Sunday, ten years after the Battle of Towton on Palm Sunday 1461, Edward stopped at Daventry to hear mass. Easter was only a week away and the appearance of having God on your side was a vital one. Whether an individual was genuinely pious enough to believe that it was important or not, it represented a propaganda weapon that could be harnessed.

The Arrival of King Edward IV records that, while hearing mass, King Edward witnessed a miracle that blessed his cause. The writer recalled that Edward frequently included St Anne, the mother of the Virgin Mary, in his prayers. St Anne was often called upon by sailors seeking protection from storms and Edward had prayed to her during their turbulent crossing from Burgundy, swearing when he landed safely to make an offering the next time he saw a statue of St Anne. The church in which Edward heard mass happened to possess an alabaster statue of St Anne.

As was traditional between Ash Wednesday and Easter Sunday, all statues and images within the church were covered or boarded up. The statue of St Anne was boarded on all sides but nevertheless Edward reportedly knelt before it to thank St Anne for his safe delivery from the storms on his crossing. As he prayed, there was a loud cracking sound and the boards around the statue split. As everyone in the church looked on in amazement, there was another loud noise as the boards broke apart and fell away from the statue. Edward made his offering and everyone with him took it as a sign that their cause was blessed.

Whether this event really happened or was invented by the writer of *The Arrival*, or whether it was a stage-managed propaganda boost to Edward's cause cannot be known for certain. The episode does demonstrate the power and importance of divine intervention and a perception of having God's backing for an enterprise. Just before he entered London, it was just what Edward needed.

67. WARWICK'S BROTHER WELCOMED KING EDWARD INTO LONDON

On 9 April 1471, Henry VI was paraded through the streets of London to whip the capital city into a frenzy and encourage them to repel the approaching army behind Edward IV. The stunt backfired spectacularly.

George Neville, Archbishop of York and younger brother of Warwick, organised the event on his brother's instruction, gathering around 6,000 men in their armour at St Paul's Cathedral to follow a route through Cheapside designed to show the king to his people. Henry himself sat atop a fine steed, but the crowds gathered to witness the spectacle were far from inspired.

King Henry cut a sorry figure, appearing bemused by his own presence at the head of the parade and instead of inspiring the citizens, his appearance caused doubt and uncertainty to spread through the crowd. Philip de Commynes offered three reasons why London was also keen to see King Edward return to power. The fact that Edward's wife and children, including his new son, who he had never met, were in sanctuary at Westminster still inspired sympathy among the people.

On a more practical note, Edward owed London merchants a fortune from his decade in power and they knew they had no hope of ever recovering that money if Edward was unsuccessful. The third reason Commynes gave was that members of the female population within London hoped for a return to Edward's bed and the rewards and prestige that brought. Women of the city worked to convince their husbands to help Edward win his throne back.

George Neville saw the way the wind was blowing. *The Arrival* insists that the majority of the clergy backed Edward and may have influenced George, but the archbishop was also trapped inside a city increasingly keen to let his enemy in. George sent secret letters to Edward asking for his pardon if the city was opened to Edward without a fight. On 10 April, the Tower of London was claimed in the name of Edward IV and on the following day Edward entered the city in triumph. George Neville led King Henry by the hand into Edward's custody and several other senior Lancastrians within the city were seized.

Edward went next to Westminster Abbey to give thanks for his victory and to liberate his family, meeting his baby son for the first time. He took Elizabeth and their children to Baynard's Castle, his mother's London home. The next day, Good Friday, Edward heard mass before gathering his council. At this point, too, Warwick marched out of Coventry towards London. An Easter confrontation seemed unavoidable.

68. Fog Caused Chaos at the Battle of Barnet

Edward IV marched out of London at the head of an army on Saturday 13 April 1471. Richard Neville, Earl of Warwick, marched south from Coventry. As darkness fell that evening, Edward ordered his men to set camp in the fields outside Barnet, perhaps wary that being caught inside a town, as had happened at St Albans, would not work in his favour. Warwick also set his camp, but neither side knew quite how close they were to each other.

Warwick had his cannons fire towards the opposition's camp but, with the distance misjudged, the shots flew over the heads of Edward's men. The king ordered his cannon to remain silent so that their proximity wasn't given away. As dawn broke on Easter Sunday, 14 April 1471, fog obscured the field between the two armies. They lined up closer to each other than was usual but also off centre because of the visibility problems. Each side's right flank overhung the opposing left flank. Edward had an estimated 10,000 men and Warwick probably around 15,000.

As the two armies marched into each other, the Earl of Oxford on Warwick's right flank quickly spotted the overlap and swung his men around to flank Lord Hastings on Edward's left flank. Hastings' men quickly broke and ran with Oxford's men in hot pursuit, cutting down the Yorkist soldiers and falling to plundering, assuming the day was won. On the opposite side of the field, Richard, Duke of Gloucester, had control of Edward's right in his first taste of battle and quickly overwhelmed the Duke of Exeter on Warwick's left.

The Earl of Warwick preferred to fight from horseback but his younger brother John had convinced him to send his horse away to demonstrate that he meant to fight with his man rather than flee. Warwick agreed and sent his horse away. Warkworth reports that as the battle raged, the fog caused more confusion when Oxford and his men finally returned. Oxford's star and streamers badge was mistaken for Edward's sunne in splendour badge and Warwick's men fired at their allies, who in turn cried treason and ran. The calls of betrayal tore through Warwick's army and they began to flee. Edward's men pressed forward and eventually won the day.

Warwick himself was overtaken just outside Barnet and killed by Edward's men, who reportedly lifted his visor and drove a dagger into his face to kill him. The Duke of Exeter was left for dead on the battlefield but later found alive by his men and rescued. Oxford escaped north and made it back to Scotland. John Neville, Marquis of Montagu, was killed and both his and his older brother's bodies were displayed at St Paul's before being buried at their family mausoleum at Bisham Priory.

Richard Neville, Earl of Warwick, entered the annals of history as 'The Kingmaker'. A powerful and proud man, he had been a friend to the House of York but died its enemy.

69. The Real Wars of the Roses Ended at the Battle of Tewkesbury

Queen Margaret and her son Edward of Westminster, Prince of Wales, landed on the south-west coast on 14 April 1471, the same day as Warwick was defeated and killed at Barnet. A large force gathered at Exeter and Margaret was able to march out of that town at the head of an army, aiming to meet up with Jasper Tudor, who was recruiting another army in Wales. There was a desperate game of cat and mouse as King Edward moved west to intercept the rest of the Lancastrian force.

On 3 May, the Lancastrian army covered a reported 36 miles in searing summer heat. The Yorkist army marched 30 miles hard on the heels of the Lancastrian forces, who were trying to cross the River Severn. The two armies made camp for the night at Tewkesbury, the Lancastrians too afraid to attempt a night crossing with the Yorkists so close behind.

On the morning of 4 May 1471, the two armies faced each other. Margaret had taken the no doubt difficult decision to allow her seventeen-year-old son to take the field, nominally in command of an army actually controlled by Edmund Beaufort, Duke of Somerset. The Yorkist cannons and archers opened fire and were better equipped than the Lancastrians. After returning fire for a while, Somerset realised they couldn't sustain the effort and ordered the attack. As Richard, Duke of Gloucester, attacked with his vanguard, Somerset led his men through a maze of pathways that allowed them to flank Edward's centre.

A small group of Edward's soldiers saw Somerset's manoeuvre and cut him off until Gloucester's vanguard attacked. Somerset's force panicked and began to flee, some drowning and others making for the abbey.

King Edward advanced on the Lancastrian centre and the battle was a close-run affair for a long time before the Yorkist force prevailed and the Lancastrians began to flee with Gloucester in pursuit. Prince Edward was killed, though precisely how and by who is uncertain. Somerset and others were dragged from the abbey and executed. In order to apologise to the brothers, Edward had the abbey redecorated with prominent sunne in splendour badges that can still be seen today. The sacristy door of the abbey is lined with horse armour recovered from the battlefield and punctured by arrow marks.

Queen Margaret was captured shortly after the battle. With the death of her only child, the Lancastrian line was doomed. On the night that Edward returned to London, King Henry died. Officially, a broken heart at the loss of his son and his cause killed the king, but it is more likely that he was murdered, perhaps by Richard, Duke of Gloucester, who was Edward's new constable. In essence, the Wars of the Roses, as a dynastic conflict between the Houses of York and Lancaster, ended in 1471 with the extinction of the legitimate Lancastrian line.

70. The Bastard of Fauconberg Sought Revenge for the Nevilles

As Edward moved to Worcester after the Battle of Tewkesbury, news arrived of an uprising in the north of worrying proportions. By the time Edward reached Coventry, Henry Percy, Earl of Northumberland, had come south to tell the king that the mere threat of his arrival had been enough to cause the threatened revolt to disband.

With Edward distracted, fresh trouble broke out in the south led by a man known as the Bastard of Fauconberg. Thomas Neville was the illegitimate son of William Neville, Warwick's uncle. William, Lord Fauconberg, had been instrumental in Edward's rise to power in 1461 and had been rewarded with the earldom of Kent. He had died peacefully in 1463 and Thomas had become a respected soldier and sailor, now in his forties. Thomas had sided with his cousin the Earl of Warwick when he fell out with King Edward and had been given command of Warwick's fleet during the readeption. Tasked with preventing Edward from crossing the Channel, storms had allowed the exiled king to slip past.

Hearing news of his cousins' defeat and death, Thomas landed and moved towards London. He was reported to have 20,000 men at his back by the time he reached London Bridge on 12 May with his fleet weighing anchor in the Thames. Warwick had left Thomas instructions that if things went badly, he was to move on London and secure the person of Henry VI. Thomas sent word that he wanted only to pass through London and move north to engage Edward, but the city kept its gates stubbornly locked.

News reached Edward in Coventry and he sent 1,500 men straight away to defend his family in the Tower on

14 May. Two days later he left himself with as many men as he could raise, though he was still outnumbered by the Bastard's force. Outraged by London's refusal to admit him, Thomas brought up cannons to begin bombarding the city. London Bridge was set alight and two forces were sent across the river in ships to attack and set fire to Bishops Gate and Aldgate. The Londoners set up cannon across the bridge so that as the smoke cleared and Thomas prepared to attack, he was met by a barricade of guns.

Anthony Woodville took a group of men out of Aldgate and attacked the Bastard's force, driving them back. Thomas pulled back and went west, hoping to cross the river. Anthony Woodville sent word to Thomas urging him to give up and leave, promising that no harm would come to him if he disbanded his army. Despite his greater numbers, Thomas turned back south, perhaps after news of Tewkesbury reached him.

Edward moved south after reaching London. Thomas sent word that he would surrender. When he received assurance of his safety, Thomas surrendered, only to be arrested and executed six months later at Richard, Duke of Gloucester's castle in Middleham.

71. EDWARD TRICKED GEORGE NEVILLE TO FINALLY CRUSH THE NEVILLE FAMILY

George Neville, Archbishop of York, had handed London and King Henry to Edward IV on his return and believed that he had escaped retribution. A year later, his illusions were to be shattered.

Warkworth's Chronicle records that in 1472, George was with King Edward at Windsor enjoying the king's hospitality, believing himself high in favour for his part in restoring Edward. George was delighted when the king informed him that he was to be honoured by a royal visit to the archbishop's manor at Moore where they would enjoy hunting together. George hurried back to make preparations, recovering all of his plate and treasure that he had put in hiding during the previous troubles to ready Moore for the king.

The day before Edward was due to visit, George received word that he was to attend upon the king at Windsor immediately. On his arrival, the archbishop was arrested and charged with aiding John de Vere, Earl of Oxford. George was sent into imprisonment at Hammes Castle near Calais and Edward despatched men to Moore to recover and confiscate all the archbishop's neatly compiled treasure.

George remained a prisoner until November 1474 when he was released, returning to England the following year. He died on 8 June 1476 in his mid-forties, escaping the fate of his brothers but never able to earn King Edward's trust again.

72. The Earl of Oxford Seized St Michael's Mount

John de Vere, Earl of Oxford, had escaped the Battle of Barnet and taken to piracy in the Channel. When he was attainted and his lands given to Richard, Duke of Gloucester, his mother was intimidated by the duke into signing over her dower lands too. This seems to have been the final straw for the desperate Oxford and he attacked.

In May 1473, Oxford attempted to land at St Osyth in Essex but was forced back from the shore. Sailing west, he finally arrived at St Michael's Mount, a tidal island fortress that was a mirror of Mont Saint-Michel off the French coast. At low tide, it was connected to the land but as the tide came back, it became an island. Oxford and around eighty men, including two of his brothers, landed at St Michael's Mount and swiftly took control of the highly defensible island.

Exactly what Oxford hoped to achieve is unclear. The Lancastrian cause was lost, though Oxford seems to have been more anti-Edward than pro-Lancastrian. He had been the most willing of the Lancastrian lords to work with Warwick and Clarence. Edward had ordered the executions of Oxford's father and older brother, making John earl, and it seems likely that Oxford never forgave the Yorkist king. The mistreatment of his mother that Edward allowed at his brother's hands might have been the final straw that drove Oxford to take desperate action and added Richard, Duke of Gloucester, to the list of men Oxford would never forgive.

By September, word reached King Edward that Oxford was moving freely about Cornwall, using St Michael's Mount as a base to recruit men. The king sent orders to Sir Henry Bodrugan, a local landowner, to deal with the problem. Bodrugan laid siege to the Mount, but word soon reached Edward that he was allowing Oxford and his men to come out each low tide, conduct a parlay and return to the fortress, even allowing them to restock when Oxford complained that their supplies were running low.

Richard Fortescu, one of Edward's squires of the body, was sent to replace Bodrugan at the end of December but was angrily confronted by the knight before being able to lay siege to the Mount properly. Almost every day there was a skirmish between the two sides at low tide, but Warkworth insisted the Mount could be defended by twenty men with ease as long as their supplies held out. During truces, Oxford's men were offered pardons and safe passage away until only a dozen men remained with the earl. On 15 February 1474, Oxford was forced to surrender St Michael's Mount, despite having plenty of supplies. He was sent to Hammes Castle at Calais where the pirate earl would remain a prisoner for a decade.

73. EDWARD IV'S INVASION OF FRANCE MARKED HIS BROTHER FOR SPECIAL ATTENTION

In 1475, Edward IV launched an invasion of France, something he had planned to do for a long time and something his brother-in-law Charles, Duke of Burgundy, supported. Together, they were going to attack Louis XI and divide the spoils of France between them. As soon as Edward landed, though, he was abandoned by Charles, who chose instead to attack the town of Neuss for little apparent reason and no gain.

The wily Louis saw an opportunity to be rid of the threat Edward posed and offered to pay the English king and his men off. Louis believed that Edward would take an easy route out if presented with one that was tempting enough. He was right. Phillip de Commynes noted that Edward had changed a great deal since the last time the two men had met, having put on weight and grown less handsome than he had been. He lacked the stomach for a long, arduous campaign and preferred Louis' offer of a huge bribe, an annual pension and a marriage for his daughter Elizabeth to Louis' son Charles.

The Treaty of Picquigny was sealed on 29 August 1475. Edward received 75,000 crowns and a pension of 50,000 crowns per year. Louis also agreed to ransom Margaret of Anjou from Edward for a further 50,000 crowns. To sweeten the deal for those who had made the expensive trip with Edward, many of his lords were also given annual pensions from the French crown.

Outside those who directly benefitted, there was dissatisfaction on both sides with the treaty. It was deemed dishonourable by many in France and England, including Louis de Bretaylle, Edward's envoy to Spain, who believed all of Edward's previous military glory had been undone in this capitulation. Richard, Duke of Gloucester, was the most senior figure to oppose the treaty on the English side. Richard refused to attend the negotiations or the sealing of the treaty, a snub that was a clear insult to both his brother and Louis. He declined the pension he was offered, though he did attend later celebrations.

Louis seems to have been intrigued by Edward's younger brother and keen to learn more about him. Richard attended a private audience with the French king at which the two talked at length and Richard accepted gifts of plate and horses. The encounter was surely designed to allow Louis to get the measure of Richard, then twenty-two and more bellicose than his brother. Louis would send Richard gifts of large cannon in the following years, no doubt keeping tabs on the duke. France was wary of Richard, Duke of Gloucester, and deeply concerned when he became Richard III. France would support Richard's enemies in 1485 in part because of his actions in 1475.

74. Henry Holland Drowned on the Return Voyage from France

Henry Holland, Duke of Exeter, had been a perennial thorn in the side of the Yorkist cause. Henry had been a ward of Richard, Duke of York, and had been married to York's oldest daughter Anne before inheriting his dukedom in 1447 at the age of seventeen.

Despite this family connection, Henry had remained utterly loyal to the Lancastrian cause throughout the period before and during the Wars of the Roses. Henry could boast of being a great-great-grandson to Edward III twice over. His father, John Holland, was the grandson of John of Gaunt, Duke of Lancaster, third son of Edward III through Gaunt's daughter Elizabeth. Henry's mother Anne Stafford was a granddaughter of Thomas of Woodstock, Duke of Gloucester, Edward III's fifth son to survive childhood through Thomas's daughter Anne.

Henry had caused constant problems for his father-in-law Richard, Duke of York, by refusing to behave as York tried to wrest power from Somerset. He played a prominent role in the Lancastrian army that defeated and killed York at the Battle of Wakefield in 1460, going on to command parts of the army at the Second Battle of St Albans in 1461 too. He managed to escape the devastating Lancastrian loss at the Battle of Towton in 1461, fleeing across the Scottish border with the remnants of the Lancastrian cause.

After Towton, Henry was attainted and all his lands and titles given to his wife Anne. The couple officially separated in 1464. The brief period of the readeption gave Henry the chance to regain his lands and titles but he was seriously wounded at the Battle of Barnet in 1471, where Warwick was defeated and killed on Edward IV's way back to the throne. Left for dead, some of his men found him after the fighting and took him away for treatment. After his recovery, he was imprisoned and Anne finally divorced him.

It is believed that Henry volunteered to take part in Edward's invasion of France in 1475, hoping to prove himself to the king now that the Lancastrian cause was ended. It was perhaps his best and only hope of rehabilitating himself after more than twenty years of opposition to a house now looking firmly settled on the throne. Henry's biggest problem may well have been Edward's need to ensure that he was rid of Lancastrian claimants. With his dual descent from Edward III, one strand flowing through John of Gaunt, Duke of Lancaster, and his previous unswerving loyalty to the Lancastrian cause, Henry represented a potential Lancastrian heir should anyone try to revive that threat against Edward, who was surely nervous of such a danger.

Henry Holland fell overboard during the voyage back from France aged forty-five. Rumours have circulated ever since that he was pushed overboard on King Edward's orders, though there is no evidence to support that assertion. He was one of the few to remain steadfast on one side, which might deserve some admiration.

75. THE METHOD OF GEORGE, DUKE OF CLARENCE'S EXECUTION IS NOT KNOWN

Isabel Neville, Duchess of Clarence, died on 22 December 1476 at the age of twenty-five, just two months after giving birth to a son named Richard, who would also not survive. Isabel's husband George, the king's brother, flew into a rage, possibly fuelled by grief. On 12 April 1477, George arrested one of Isabel's ladies, Ankarette Twynyho, accusing her of poisoning her mistress, though it is widely believed that Isabel succumbed to tuberculosis.

Ankarette was arrested in Somerset and taken to Bath, then on to Cirencester the following day and on the third day she was in Warwick, George's main seat of power. Thrown into a cell, her daughter and son-in-law, who had followed her north, were expelled from Warwick by George, having to lodge at Stratford-upon-Avon. At 9 o'clock the next morning, Ankarette was hauled before the duke to be tried. A jury, who would later insist they had been threatened by George, found her guilty. By midday, she had been sentenced to death and she was quickly taken through Warwick to the gallows at Myton where she was hanged.

King Edward had a very real problem. George had exercised an authority he did not hold and it was just the latest in a long line of betrayals since 1469. Matters were oddly brought to a head when John Stacy, described by the *Crowland Chronicle* as a 'great sorcerer', and an accomplice, Thomas Burdet, were hanged for using sorcery to try and bring about the death of Richard, Lord Beauchamp, for his unfaithful wife. The day after their executions, George burst into a council meeting accompanied by Dr William Goddard, a prominent Lancastrian, and ordered Goddard to read aloud the last speeches of Stacy and Burdet and condemning their treatment. It was rich of George to criticise royal justice after what he had done.

When Edward heard what George had done, he ordered him to come to Windsor where the king arrested his brother and placed him in the Tower of London. When Parliament met in early 1478, Edward brought charges of treason against his brother, claiming 'a conspiracy against him, the queen, their son and heir and a great part of the nobility of the land has recently come to his knowledge, which treason is more heinous and unnatural than any previous one because it originates from the king's brother the duke of Clarence, whom the king had always loved and generously rewarded'. The duke was attainted and sentenced to death.

On 18 February 1478, George, Duke of Clarence, was executed, aged twenty-eight. The sentence was carried out in private, a right of his rank, and no record of the method of execution exists. A story later emerged that George had been permitted to choose the method of his execution and had elected to be drowned in a butt of malmsey wine, Edward's favourite drink, but there is no definitive evidence to support or disprove the story.

76. Richard, Duke of Gloucester's Attack on Scotland Was Hailed as a Success and a Failure

A fragile truce between England and Scotland expired in 1481 and as France prepared to renege on the Treaty of Picquigny with England too, the French king Louis XI encouraged James III of Scotland to begin causing trouble on the northern border of their mutual enemy. A response was needed from England.

Edward IV began preparations to raise an army and take it north but he appears to have lacked the physical conditioning and the will to make the long journey on campaign. After the death of the Earl of Warwick, much of his vast northern estates had gone to Richard, Duke of Gloucester, Edward's youngest brother, who had also married Warwick's younger daughter Anne Neville. Richard had become something of a champion in the region, winning tax breaks from his brother and keeping the Scottish border area more peaceful than it had been for some time. The king took the decision in 1482 to pass command of the operation against Scotland to his brother.

The campaign took on the traditional format. The Scots withdrew and hid, taking livestock and supplies with them as the English harried and burned towns and villages to try and provoke a confrontation. When the English ran out of supplies, they would be forced to head back across the border and the Scots would emerge from hiding. This time, Richard did not turn back but pushed on to Edinburgh. Richard's army entered the capital and the Scots were forced to sue for peace. By the time Richard got back to the border, Berwick-upon-Tweed had been won back and has remained on the English side of the border ever since.

King Edward wrote to Pope Sixtus IV, 'Thank God, the giver of all good gifts, for the support received from our most loving brother, whose success is so proven that he alone would suffice to chastise the whole kingdom of Scotland. This year we appointed our very dear brother Richard Duke of Gloucester to command the same army which we ourselves intended to have led last year, had not adverse turmoil hindered us ... The noble band of victors, however, spared the supplicant and prostrate citizens, the churches, and not only the widows, orphans, and minors, but all persons found there unarmed.'

However, the *Crowland Chronicler*, politically well-informed but no fan of Richard, wrote rather that 'this trifling, I really know not whether to call it "gain" or "loss," (for the safe keeping of Berwick each year swallows up ten thousand marks), at this period diminished the resources of king and kingdom by more than a hundred thousand pounds. King Edward was vexed at this frivolous outlay of so much money, although the recovery of Berwick above-mentioned in some degree alleviated his sorrow. These were the results of the duke's expeditions into Scotland in the summer of the year of our Lord, 1482'.

77. When Edward IV Died, Peace Was Still Fragile

Edward IV died on 9 April 1483 a few weeks before his forty-first birthday. It is believed that he caught a chill while fishing, though there has been frequent speculation since that his wife's family were to blame for his sudden death. Edward and Elizabeth Woodville had eight surviving children together and the king had several illegitimate children too. He had reportedly put on a great deal of weight, lost his good looks and his interest in government. It had been twelve years since the last battle for his crown, but just beneath the surface, division still threatened Yorkist England.

Edward had been negotiating with Lady Margaret Beaufort, wife of Lord Stanley, to find a way to allow her son Henry Tudor to return from twelve years in exile in Brittany with his uncle Jasper Tudor, former Earl of Pembroke. Henry and Jasper represented the last openly unreconciled vestige of Lancastrian sympathy. Edward was considering a return to their earldoms of Richmond and Pembroke, respectively, and a match for Henry to one of his daughters. Whether the wily and careful Tudors believed the offer was genuine or carried a threat is unclear, as Edward's death ended the negotiations.

Perhaps the most threatening dissent lay within Edward's own close circle. *Grafton's Chronicle*, compiled in the mid-sixteenth century and happy to place words into the mouths of historical figures that cannot be proven, nevertheless paints a picture in which Edward was well aware of the threat posed by the feud between his wife's family and a court party focussed around his close friend Lord Hastings. Grafton has Edward pleading with his stepson Thomas Grey, Marquis of Dorset, and Lord Hastings in particular to unite for the sake of his twelve-year-old son and heir Edward. Pleading with the men to mend their differences, which appears to have included sharing a mistress of Edward's, the king dies having appointed his brother Richard, Duke of Gloucester, to be Protector of the Realm during the new king's minority.

Edward's concerns were soon realised as the queen's family attempted to use their prominent position on the Council to bypass a protectorate and have the new king crowned and declared of age quickly. Lord Hastings wrote to Richard warning him of what was happening and in that air of suspicion, when Richard met his nephew's entourage moving from Ludlow to London, the duke arrested Anthony Woodville, Earl Rivers, the queen's brother, along with Sir Richard Grey, her younger son, from her first marriage and Sir Thomas Vaughan, the new king's chamberlain. The men were transferred to Richard's strongholds in the north and the queen and her other children went into sanctuary in Westminster Abbey.

King for twenty-two years, apart from six months of the readeption, the peace Edward IV had built was still fragile and dependent upon the glue of his personality to keep it together. It was to be tested earlier than Edward would have liked.

78. EDWARD V ARRIVED IN LONDON ON THE DATE SET FOR HIS CORONATION

The Council had set a date for the coronation of Edward V. With the queen's family applying pressure to see it done quickly, arrangements began for the ceremony to take place on 4 May 1483, adding to the suspicion that they meant to try and exclude Richard, Duke of Gloucester, and proceed to a coronation before he arrived from the far north.

When Richard, aided by Henry Stafford, Duke of Buckingham, arrested those closest to Edward V at Stony Stratford, he sent a shockwave through those arrangements. The queen took sanctuary in Westminster Abbey and her brother was sent north as a prisoner, perhaps meant as a hostage for her good behaviour.

Rather than being crowned on 4 May 1483, that was the date that Edward finally arrived in London, clearly marking Richard's determined policy to slow things down, which has since fuelled speculation that he was planning a coup by this point. The new king wore blue velvet as he rode into the capital flanked by his uncle Richard and the Duke of Buckingham, both in mourning black. Richard installed his nephew at the Bishop of London's Palace and tried to calm the capital by bringing all the Lords Spiritual and Temporal currently in the city before the new king to swear their allegiance.

Before leaving the north, Richard had overseen a funeral mass for his brother, the king, and caused the senior members of the community there to swear fealty to his nephew. If Richard was planning to make a bid for power at this point, causing such men to swear public oaths of loyalty was a dangerous step for him because such oaths would not easily be broken in the future. The main reason Richard's father had been unable to dislodge Henry VI from the throne was, according to those in Parliament, the frequent and recent swearing of oaths of loyalty to him so that even if he was not the correct king, their oaths could not be broken. Gloucester, however, may have been aware of his father's argument that such an oath cannot override the law of God, nor excuse men from doing what is right. If he was planning to seize power, this would be his way out of the oaths that would buy him time. It was risky, though, if that was his plan. His father had not been made king, only heir, and few in London appeared to doubt Richard's sincerity at this point.

The coming weeks would be a muddled and controversial period in which motives are hard to discern but which would relight the fuse of civil war.

79. The Lord Protector Was Not the Head of Government

During the medieval period, several nations, including France, had frequent regencies headed by women, usually the king's mother or sister. Although Salic Law in France prohibited succession through the female line, a female regency during a minority or incapacity was considered normal. This cultural difference may have led to Margaret of Anjou's attempt to claim power in 1454 when Henry VI was taken ill.

England had never seen a female regent and the deeply misogynistic English society was not prepared to consider one. When Elizabeth Woodville appeared to be making a bid for authority during her son's minority, it would not have been widely welcomed, in part because the Woodville family had become disliked but also because the queen appeared to be seeking the reins of government.

In constitutional terms, England had a blueprint for this situation. Henry V had died when his son, Henry VI, was just nine months old, necessitating a long minority. In his will, Henry V set out his vision but it was altered after his death. What emerged was a three-way division of responsibility. The person of the king, his protection and education were placed into the hands of one party. The position of Protector of the Realm held responsibility for military affairs, both domestic and abroad, and the government was carried out by the Council, though it was considered proper that the Protector should take a prominent role on the Council too.

In 1422, Richard Beauchamp, Earl of Warwick, was given responsibility for the education of Henry VI. With John, Duke of Bedford, preoccupied in France, Henry V's other brother Humphrey, Duke of Gloucester, was made Protector of the Realm and the Council dealt with the day-to-day business of government. This situation was recreated in 1454 when Henry VI was taken ill, with Queen Margaret having responsibility for the king's care, Richard, Duke of York, acting as Protector and the Council governing.

When Edward appointed his brother Richard Protector in 1483, he did not do so to give Richard the powers of a regent. Anthony Woodville had responsibility for the new king. The Council would continue to govern, though it would have been unusual if Richard were not at the head of that Council as the senior male adult of the blood royal. Richard was given primary responsibility for security. The duke had proven himself an effective commander and soldier in 1471 and in 1482 when he led a campaign against Scotland. With the Scots still unsettled, Louis XI repudiating the Treaty of Picquigny in a clearly aggressive move and Henry Tudor trying to get home, Edward recognised the need for a Protector in 1483.

By arresting Anthony Woodville at Stony Stratford, Richard disrupted this tripartite arrangement, but he was still legally only a member of government, not the sole leader of it. Even in death, security eluded Edward IV's government.

80. Richard, Duke of Gloucester, Lost His Security Just When He Needed It

George Neville, the disinherited son of John Neville, Marquis Montagu, Warwick's brother, died on 4 May 1483 in his early twenties after a brief illness. He was unmarried and had no children. At any time it was a sad tragedy, but happening when it did made an already complex situation even more difficult.

When the Neville inheritance was split after Warwick's death between King Edward's brothers George and Richard, the king inserted a clause designed to protect the remaining Neville male heir, George, then Duke of Bedford, but denied the title in 1478. Warwick's widow, Anne Beauchamp, was declared legally dead by Parliament so that she could be dispossessed and her daughters, married to Edward's brothers, could inherit as if she had died. On 23 February 1473, Parliament had sealed Richard's grant of his share of the Neville lands, but included a clause that stated:

> Also it is ordained by the said authority that if the said male issue begotten or coming of the body of the said John Neville, knight, die without male issue coming of their bodies while the said duke is alive, that the said duke shall then have and enjoy all the things stated for term of his life.

When George Neville, the only son of John, died without issue on 4 May 1483, the same day Richard entered London with his nephew Edward V; this clause was activated to devastating effect. It meant that Richard's interest in a large part of his estates reverted to a life interest only. His son would never inherit these lands and on his death, they would revert to the king.

Richard may have hoped to work on his brother, the king, to improve this situation, but Edward's death denied him the opportunity. With the Woodville family of the queen apparently working to exclude Richard and retain their influence by having Edward crowned quickly, the prospect of regaining this inheritance must have seemed remote and just as he became Protector, his own position was significantly weakened when he needed to be able to operate from a position of strength.

Richard wrote to the city of York on 10 June asking them to send soldiers to help him as quickly as possible, 'to aid and assist us against the Queen, her blood adherents and affinity,' because Richard feared they sought to destroy him and all those of the 'old royal blood of this realm'. This has often been seen as an act of aggression, part of Richard's plot to snatch power, but it might well have been a defensive reaction to events that were unfolding, not only in London but in Richard's personal situation too.

81. Lord Hastings' Execution Was Not Illegal

Events at the Tower of London on 13 June 1483 were to prove infamous and decisive. There might have been clues for those involved that something was awry. As the majority of the council met elsewhere, Richard, Duke of Gloucester, Henry Stafford, Duke of Buckingham, William, Lord Hastings, Thomas, Lord Stanley, John Morton, Bishop of Ely, and Thomas Rotherham, Bishop of Rochester, met at the Tower in a separate meeting, nominally to finalise arrangements for the coronation of Edward V.

The events that followed have been dramatized by Sir Thomas More in his *The History of King Richard the Third*, still considered a definitive factual account of events by many despite it numerous and obvious errors. Richard cried treason, had all but Buckingham arrested and ordered Lord Hastings' immediate execution in the Tower grounds. The traditional interpretation of the events of that day are that it was a cynical ploy by Richard to eliminate Edward V's chief support to prepare for his own bid for the throne, clearly signalling that this was Richard's plan by this point, and furthermore that the execution of Lord Hastings was rushed, without trial and therefore unlawful.

Another version of these events offers a different view. The later version of events in 1483 that usually seek to vilify Richard almost all offer an insight into the matter of Hastings' execution. Polydore Virgil wrote during Henry VII's reign that after Richard took custody of Edward V at Stony Stratford, which Hastings had advised the duke to do, Lord Hastings 'called together unto Paul's church such friends as he knew to be right careful for the life, dignity, and estate of prince Edward, and conferred with them what best was to be done'. Here, Virgil portrays Hastings whipping up sentiment against Richard even before he arrived in London.

Grafton, a Tudor antiquary, wrote that the night before the council meeting, 'Lord Stanley sent to him [Hastings] a trusty and secret messenger at midnight in all the haste, requiring him to rise and ride away with him' and More goes on to explain that Catesby, a lawyer, who worked for Lord Hastings, had brought Richard news of Hastings' actions, describing 'Catesby's account of the Lord Hastings's words and discourse, which he so represented to him, as if he had wished and contrived his death'.

Grafton reported that Richard told Hastings 'by Saint Paul, I will not dine till I see thy head off' and that afterwards Richard summoned the aldermen and showed them evidence 'that the Lord Hastings and other of his conspiracy had contrived to have suddenly destroyed him and the Duke of Buckingham there the same day in council'. These hostile sources seem to agree that Hastings might have been working against Richard. As Constable of England, Richard was entitled to try cases of treason on evidence he had seen, acting as judge and jury. Whatever his motives, if Richard had the proof he showed the aldermen, Lord Hastings' execution was not an illegal act.

82. Edward V Was Declared Illegitimate

The last date ever set for the coronation of Edward V was 22 June 1483. That coronation never took place. Instead, on that day, Dr Ralph Shaa, half-brother of the Mayor of London, preached a sermon at St Paul's Cross entitled 'Bastard Slips Shall Not Take Deep Root', which changed everything.

Philippe de Commynes, a Burgundian chronicler, reported that Robert Stillington, Bishop of Bath and Wells, came to Richard with news that he had officiated over a pre-contract to marry between Edward IV and Lady Eleanor Talbot. Crucially, this had happened before Edward's marriage to Elizabeth Woodville and although Eleanor Talbot had died in 1468, she had been alive in 1464 when Edward had married Elizabeth. A pre-contract to marry was, in medieval canon law, a legally binding arrangement as good as an actual marriage. Since Edward had allegedly not had this arrangement dissolved, the news would have meant that his marriage to Elizabeth Woodville was bigamous and the children of their union illegitimate and unable to inherit.

The truth of this claim is impossible to establish. Was it possible that Edward IV had been party to a clandestine marriage in order to get a lady into his bed? Absolutely. That is how he came to be married to Elizabeth Woodville. His carnal reputation had helped him regain power in 1471 but was about to cost his son the crown.

Dr Shaa made the claim public, including some allusion to Edward IV's own legitimacy that had been an old story used by Warwick and Clarence that appeared to originate from Louis XI's court in France. This portion was quickly dropped, whether for lack of truth, evidence or will to upset Richard's mother. Bishop Stillington reportedly produced evidence to a group of lords gathered in London in preparation for the coronation and Parliament that was due to open afterwards. These men were apparently satisfied with what they saw and declared Edward V illegitimate, though importantly they were not assembled as a Parliament yet so the declaration was potentially somewhat flawed.

On 25 June, at Baynards Castle, his mother's London residence, Richard was petitioned by the mayor, aldermen and those who had arrived for the planned Parliament to take the throne as the only available legitimate male heir of the House of York. What purports to be a copy of the document was later enacted by Parliament as Titulus Regius, outlining Richard's legal title due to the illegitimacy of Edward IV's children and the attainder against George, Duke of Clarence, that excluded his son Edward and daughter Margaret from the succession. Richard was asked to become king, but the question has always been as simple as it is impossible to answer. Was Richard telling the truth, or lying to get the crown?

83. THE CORONATION OF RICHARD III AND QUEEN ANNE WAS THE FIRST JOINT CORONATION IN 175 YEARS

London had been preparing for a coronation, but not for the one that took place on 6 July 1483. Instead of Edward V, the ceremony sanctified the kingship of Richard III. At his side was his wife, Anne Neville. It was only the fourth joint coronation since the Conquest and the first in 175 years.

The absence for so long of a couple being crowned together was in part a testament to the upheavals of the previous century or more. Edward III had taken his father's throne at a young age. His heir had died less than a year before he was to, leaving his ten-year-old grandson to reign. Richard II was to be punished for his tyranny when the widowed Henry IV removed him. Henry died aged forty-six, leaving his unmarried son to be crowned Henry V. When that warrior-king died, his son was only nine months old. Henry VI's insipid rule brought about the Wars of the Roses and saw Edward IV seize the throne, crowned at nineteen before he met Elizabeth Woodville. It was his son, aged twelve, who had been due to be crowned on 22 June. So perhaps this joint coronation of a settled, mature couple, Richard being thirty and Anne aged twenty-seven, promised much, the couple also having a son and heir ready to act as Prince of Wales.

The spectacle proper began as the king and queen processed from Westminster Hall to Westminster Abbey. They walked barefoot, as was traditional, behind a large cross and members of the clergy. Henry Percy, Earl of Northumberland, carried the blunt sword of mercy. Thomas, Lord Stanley, bore the Lord High Constable's mace. Next came the Earl of Kent and Richard's closest friend Francis, Viscount Lovell, each carrying a pointed sword of justice. Richard's brother-in-law, the Duke of Suffolk, held the sceptre and the king's nephew, John de la Pole, Earl of Lincoln, bore the cross and ball. Thomas Howard, Earl of Surrey, solemnly bore the sheathed sword of state held upright before him. Finally came Surrey's father, John Howard, Duke of Norfolk, carefully holding the crown in his hands.

King Richard himself walked enrobed in a sumptuous purple velvet gown, a bishop at each shoulder and his train born by the Duke of Buckingham. The Wardens of the Cinque Ports held the cloth of estate above the king's head. The luxury and vivid, vibrant colours would have been a sight to behold and the message of a bright new future clear for all to see.

Behind followed a series of earls, barons and lords bearing the queen's regalia. Anne walked behind with Margaret Beaufort, Countess of Richmond, holding her train. Richard's sister Elizabeth, Duchess of Suffolk, walked alone in state followed by a further twenty ladies of the nobility and a host of knights and squires.

It must have seemed a promising beginning.

84. A POORLY RECORDED ATTEMPT TO FREE THE PRINCES IN THE TOWER MIGHT HAVE FORCED RICHARD TO ACT

There is believed to have been an attack on the Tower of London, possibly in late June or early July, aimed at freeing the Princes in the Tower. It is not clear whether the attack was instigated by the Woodville faction or another group, or indeed, whether the rescue attempt even certainly took place.

If the Tower was attacked, the boys do not appear to have been liberated. It has been suggested that they could have been injured or even killed during a botched rescue bid. It has also been suggested that the attack might have spurred Richard to deal with the boys once and for all. If Richard did feel that he had to act, the question was whether he would have chosen to kill his nephews, or have them hidden away from view.

The fate of the boys known as the Princes in the Tower is one of the most enduring and fascinating mysteries in history. If this attack took place, it might have sealed their fates, though precisely what those fates were remains tantalisingly beyond knowledge.

85. Buckingham's Rebellion Was Undone by the Weather

Richard III was only king for five months before he faced a serious threat to his rule. Henry Stafford, Duke of Buckingham, had been a key figure in Richard's propulsion to the throne, but he would soon be named by his king 'the most untrue creature living'.

Buckingham was given custody of John Morton, Bishop of Ely, after Lord Hastings' execution at the Tower and took the bishop to his castle at Brecknock in Wales. The Tudor antiquarian Edward Hall claimed that Buckingham met Margaret Beaufort at Bridgnorth on his way to Wales and the two discussed the return of her son Henry Tudor. Given the involvement of Margaret and Bishop Morton in Henry Tudor's return and seizure of the throne, it seems feasible that this was the beginning of turning Buckingham away from Richard.

Another key factor of the uprising was that it began with the stated purpose of releasing and restoring Edward V but, with rumours of the death of both sons of Edward IV, which the *Crowland Chronicle* claims originated as part of the uprising, the objective changed to placing Henry Tudor on the throne – potentially an odd aim when Buckingham's claim was better than Henry's. As part of this arrangement, Elizabeth Woodville apparently agreed from sanctuary to allow her oldest daughter Elizabeth to marry Henry. Crucially, this suggests that she believed her sons were dead, though one of her few sources of information was Margaret Beaufort's physician Dr Lewis Caerleon.

The revolt was due to be activated on 18 October 1483, the Feast of St Luke, with men from Kent attacking London to draw Richard in, at which point forces would attack from the West Country, Wiltshire and Berkshire with Buckingham leading his men out of Wales.

Henry Tudor would land on the south coast with Breton archers and together they would fall upon Richard's back. The threat was broad and very real.

There was a misfire when men from Kent marched to London on 10 October, eight days early. John Howard, Duke of Norfolk, captured several of the rebels and extracted from them details of the uprising allowing Richard to prepare. Bridges over the River Severn were broken to stop Buckingham crossing and as heavy rain began to fall, his men deserted his cause. Storms in the Channel scattered Henry Tudor's fleet and when he finally neared the shore, soldiers beckoned him with word of the revolt's success, but Henry was suspicious and turned back to Brittany.

On 12 October, Richard dictated a letter to his Chancellor, Bishop John Russell, referring to Buckingham as 'him that had best cause to be true, the Duke of Buckingham, the most untrue creature living; whom with God's grace we shall not be long till that we will be in those parts, and subdue his malice'. On 2 November, Buckingham was beheaded in Salisbury marketplace and disaster for Richard was averted.

86. MARGARET BEAUFORT GOT AWAY WITH TREASON

Following Henry Tudor's attempt to invade England in October 1483, his mother was placed under house arrest and when Parliament met in 1484, the matter of her treason was brought before the session. The leniency she was shown is perhaps surprising, except that the execution of noble women was a rarity before Margaret's grandson Henry VIII's reign.

An act appears in the Parliament Rolls for the attainder of Margaret, Countess of Richmond, detailing her part in the October uprising and the help she offered her son Henry Tudor, 'in particular by sending messages, writings and tokens to the said Henry, urging, instigating and stirring him by them to come into this realm to make war upon our said sovereign lord', adding that she had 'supplied great sums of money' and had 'conspired, leagued and plotted the destruction of our said sovereign lord, and knew of and assented to, and assisted in the treason planned and committed by Henry, late duke of Buckingham, and his supporters'.

However, the attainder was not enacted, the Parliament Rolls giving the reason as Richard's 'special grace, mindful of the good and faithful service which Thomas, Lord Stanley, has given'. Margaret's husband had won her a reprieve, as the Parliament Rolls record that Richard 'remits and will forbear the great punishment of attainting the said countess', deciding rather to confiscate all of her property and grant it to Lord Stanley, her husband, making him responsible for her good behaviour.

The episode demonstrates several important facts. Firstly, it was still considered improper to deal harshly with a noble woman, even one so steeped in treason as Margaret was and even for a man considered as evil as

Richard III is by many. Secondly, it shows that Thomas, Lord Stanley, was high in Richard's favour and trust, despite being involved in the incident at the Tower in which Lord Hastings was executed.

Richard's failure to enact the attainder also demonstrates a lack of political astuteness that is a trait he never overcame. Blunt and intractable, Richard appeared to expect the same openness in others. The continued work of Margaret in her son's cause and Lord Stanley's eventual betrayal of Richard at Bosworth suggest that the king was unwise to be so lenient with the couple, particularly as Margaret's son remained committed to marrying Elizabeth of York, daughter of Edward IV, and to taking Richard's throne.

87. Queen Anne Died On the Day of a Solar Eclipse

Queen Anne, Richard's wife of over ten years, died at the age of twenty-eight on 16 March 1485. The day was marked by a solar eclipse that was deemed an ill omen for her husband's reign.

The couple had lost their only child, Edward of Middleham, Prince of Wales, in April 1484, causing problems with the succession. The *Crowland Chronicle* reports that 'on hearing the news of this, at Nottingham, where they were then residing, you might have seen his father and mother in a state almost bordering on madness, by reason of their sudden grief'. For Richard, the loss of his wife less than a year later was a personal tragedy, but also a dynastic threat. He had been transformed from a married man with a son and heir into a single thirty-two-year-old with no legitimate children.

Rumours began to spring up that Richard had poisoned his wife in order to allow him to marry his own niece, Elizabeth of York, who had been claimed by Henry Tudor. Richard was forced to make a public and embarrassing denial that he planned to marry his brother's daughter, but the rumours have stuck ever since.

It is likely that Anne died of consumption – tuberculosis – rather than having been poisoned by Richard. The king had begun negotiations for a marriage to Joanna of Portugal, daughter of Alfonso V. The negotiations included a match between Elizabeth of York and Joanna's cousin Manuel, who would later become Manuel I. The negotiations were left incomplete when Richard was killed at the Battle of Bosworth, but the fact that they were in progress perhaps before Anne died, when it became clear that her illness was terminal, does not support the notion that Richard wanted to marry his niece.

George Buck, a seventeenth-century writer who sought to re-evaluate the reputation of Richard III, recorded a letter that he had seen but which no longer survives that he believed was written by Elizabeth of York to John Howard, Duke of Norfolk, asking him 'to be a mediator' for her to Richard in the cause of her marriage to him, describing her uncle as 'her only joy and maker in this world, and that she was his in heart and in thoughts, in body and in all' before callously remarking that 'she feared the Queen would never die'. It is possible that Elizabeth had feelings for her uncle or even that, as part of the plot with Margaret Beaufort and Henry Tudor her mother had subscribed to, Elizabeth was writing to Richard's closest supporters to initiate a scandal. Sir Richard Ratcliffe and Sir William Catesby, both very close to the king, reportedly approached Richard to advise him to publicly deny the story and it may be possible that they received similar letters as part of a campaign to discredit and dislodge Richard as tragedy struck his personal life.

88. Henry Tudor Narrowly Avoided Being Sent To Richard III in 1485

The life of Henry Tudor is an incredible story of loss, hardship, extraordinary gain and personal tragedy. His father had died before he was born, his mother had been thirteen at the time of his birth on a stormy night at Pembroke Castle on 28 January 1457. Placed in the household of his father's enemy, William Herbert, who was given Henry's uncle Jasper's title of Earl of Pembroke, Henry was well treated but separated from his mother. The brief readeption of Henry VI had given the young Henry a brief moment of reconciliation with his mother before the return of Edward IV saw him forced into exile in Brittany with his uncle Jasper in 1471.

In October 1483, Henry had tried to land in England as part of the uprising remembered as Buckingham's Rebellion. When soldiers had beckoned him ashore with news of the success of the uprising, Henry's by then natural suspicion and instinct for self-preservation had caused him to doubt the news and turn away. On Christmas Day 1483, he swore an oath at Rennes Cathedral to marry Elizabeth of York, oldest daughter of Edward IV, and take Richard III's throne. After twelve years in exile, he had set himself on a collision course with the House of York as the last heir of the House of Lancaster.

Francis II, Duke of Brittany, had kept Jasper and Henry Tudor in comfortable confinement, using them as bargaining chips between France and England, who both sought custody of the men. In 1485, the duke's health was failing and his government was being run by Pierre Landlais, his chief minister. Pierre made a deal with Richard, which included a hefty bribe for himself, that would see Henry handed over to Richard. Bishop John Morton, also in exile on the Continent after the failed uprising of 1483, appears to have discovered news of the deal and warned Henry, who managed to slip away from those meant to escort him to the coast and escape across the border to France.

Louis XI had died a few months after Edward IV, leaving his son to become Charles VIII of France at the age of thirteen. Louis may well have marked Richard as a potential threat, keen on war with France, and members of Charles' government would have been aware of that view. Henry Tudor, grandson of Catherine of Valois, possessed more French royal blood than English and although Salic Law prevented inheritance through the female line in France, Edward III had begun the Hundred Years War on the basis that a claim could be passed down a female line. Henry was greeted in Paris disingenuously as the legitimate second son of Henry VI to bolster his claim to the throne of England, and also, perhaps, to keep Henry's eye off the French throne.

Henry had achieved another lucky escape and his time was fast approaching.

89. John de Vere Broke Out of Prison to Join Henry Tudor

The Lancastrian cause suddenly burst back into life after more than a decade in the shadows. After as long in prison, John de Vere, Earl of Oxford, sprang back to the forefront of English politics too. He had been a prisoner since being forced to end his seizure of St Michael's Mount in 1473. Shortly after the execution of George, Duke of Clarence, John had jumped from the walls of Hammes Castle. It is uncertain whether he was making a bid for freedom or attempting to take his own life. Oxford had been willing to work with Clarence and the House of Lancaster, but both were lost. He seems to have hated Edward with a passion and clearly held no love for Richard III.

Henry Tudor was running a court in exile with steadfast Lancastrians and disaffected Yorkists, who had thrived under Edward IV and disapproved of Richard III, swelling his numbers. One thing that he sorely lacked was military experience. Henry had none beyond his training. Jasper Tudor had been involved in a handful of battles but was not really a recognised general. If Henry was to launch a second invasion he was going to need someone with military credentials to help his cause.

After Henry's escape from Brittany to France, John de Vere, Earl of Oxford, made a bid to join the court in exile after more than a decade as a prisoner of the Yorkist state at Hammes Castle near Calais. Somehow, John managed to convince the Captain of Hammes Castle, James Blount, not only to allow him to leave his prison but also to join him. Blount's deputy John Fortescue joined them and the majority of the castle's garrison were ordered to leave for France with their captain.

Richard III was understandably furious. He offered a pardon to any members of the garrison who returned to their duties quickly and most did. The lure of a regular wage from the crown was probably a far more appealing proposition than the fragility of a court in exile that may never be able to make a move. Richard was no doubt also worried by the development. Tudor had lacked a general to organise his forces and lead them onto a battlefield. He now had one of the most militarily experienced Englishmen alive in his camp. It was a real boost to Henry Tudor's cause and a blow to Richard, who could not even keep a high value prisoner in jail.

France was taking Henry Tudor seriously as a claimant to the English throne. Richard was now forced to do the same. The final piece of Henry's jigsaw of opposition was in place and France was offering men and funding for an invasion.

90. Henry Tudor Landed at Mill Bay and Recited Psalm 43

After fourteen years in exile and one failed attempt to invade England, Henry Tudor sailed from Harfleur on 1 August 1485 with around 2,000 men made up of Lancastrian loyalists, Yorkist dissidents and French mercenaries. He landed at Mill Bay near Milford Haven on the south-west coast of Wales on 7 August 1485, falling to his knees on the shore and reciting Psalm 43: 'Judge me, Oh Lord, and defend my cause'.

The area in which Henry landed was under the authority of Rhys ap Thomas, promoted by Richard to be Principal Lieutenant in south-west Wales. It has been reported that Rhys had sworn an oath to King Richard that 'whoever ill-fated to the state, shall dare to land in these parts of Wales where I have employment under your majesty, must resolve with himself to make his entrance and irruption over my belly'. In order to absolve himself from this vow and save embarrassment, the story goes that Rhys stood under a bridge as Henry walked over it, so that Henry made his entry into Wales over Rhys's belly.

Henry began his march north along the coast of Wales but men were slow to come to his cause. Rhys only joined his army near the English border and they marched on to meet Richard III's army near Market Bosworth.

91. Richard III Was the Last King of England to Die in Battle

Richard III arrayed his army on the morning of 22 August 1485. It is believed he took a position on top of Ambion Hill, giving him the high ground and a good view of the field. Richard had led 6,000 men from Leicester to the battlefield and Henry Percy, Earl of Northumberland, brought 3,000 men to the king's side. Henry Tudor's force had swollen from the 2,000 he left France with to around 5,000 men. Thomas, Lord Stanley, had pledged to fight for Richard, though the king kept Stanley's son as a hostage to ensure his father's good behaviour. Stanley had also reportedly met with Henry Tudor the night before the battle and pledged his sword to his stepson's cause. With around 4,000 men at his back, Stanley had the potential to swing the day and probably knew it.

John de Vere, Earl of Oxford, led Henry's army onto the field. Henry himself remained at the rear, allowing the experienced Oxford to command. John Howard, Duke of Norfolk, led the vanguard of the king's army, Richard himself controlling the centre and perhaps uncharacteristically stepping back from the front line. Cannon fire and archery opened the battle and then the two forces came together. Norfolk was killed in the fighting and his son was injured. At this point, it is believed that Richard ordered Northumberland to advance, but the earl's men did not move. He would later blame marshy ground for blocking his path, but there has been suspicion also that Northumberland decided to betray Richard.

The king at this point spied Henry Tudor's banner and a small group of men moving across the rear of the battlefield towards Lord Stanley's position. With things going badly wrong, he ordered a charge of his household knights across the field to intercept Tudor, who was presumed to be moving to implore Lord Stanley to intervene on his behalf. The thundering charge of a group of knights on their destriers with lances couched and visors lowered must have been a sight to behold.

Richard came very close to Henry Tudor in the melee that followed. The king unhorsed Sir John Cheney, a giant of a man, a feat made all the more impressive by the revelation that Richard had serious scoliosis that restricted his movement and breathing. William Brandon, Henry's standard bearer, was killed, suggesting that the fighting was very close, since the standard was supposed to remain at Henry's side.

At this point, Lord Stanley saw his opportunity to affect the battle. He ordered his younger brother Sir William to attack Richard's men and the king was surrounded and killed. The remains discovered in Leicester revealed eleven wounds inflicted around the time of his death, the fatal strike probably coming from a halberd blow that cut away the back of Richard's skull. The battle was won by Henry Tudor, who was proclaimed Henry VII. Richard's body was further mutilated and hurriedly buried at the Greyfriars in Leicester.

92. Hornby Castle Might Have Cost Richard III the Battle of Bosworth

As the dispute between Edward IV and the Earl of Warwick intensified, local feuds began to erupt once more in the vacuum of authority. The Paston Letters detail the problems the family experienced when a local contact of theirs, Sir John Fastolf, left Caister Castle to Sir John Paston in his will. John Mowbray, Duke of Norfolk, began legal proceedings to claim the castle but as law and order broke down, Norfolk took cannons to Caister to blast the Pastons out, eventually taking and keeping the castle.

One of the other feuds that erupted may have seemed unremarkable on the surface but had an impact on the course of the Wars of the Roses fifteen years later. Two great families in Lancashire, the Stanley and Harrington families, found themselves rubbing up against each other. The Stanley family were particularly vociferous in their growth, led by the same Lord Stanley who had narrowly avoided an attainder in 1459. The same lawlessness that saw Caister Castle besieged allowed Lord Stanley to pursue his claim to Hornby Castle.

The Harringtons had been loyal to the House of York from early in their opposition to Henry VI. Thomas Harrington and his oldest son John had fought alongside the king's father Richard, Duke of York, at the Battle of Wakefield. Thomas had reportedly died in the fighting and John of his wounds shortly afterwards. Crucially, this meant that on Thomas's death, his lands passed to John and then on John's death to his two daughters. This made them incredibly eligible young girls and meant that Hornby would leave the Harrington family. Thomas's other sons James and Robert claimed their brother had died before their father so that the inheritance was James's but to no avail. Wardship of John's oldest daughter Anne was granted to another family along with her marriage rights so that James and Robert took their nieces and dug themselves in at Hornby Castle.

When James and Robert appeared in the Court of Chancery to answer for their actions, Lord Stanley applied to King Edward for and was granted custody of both girls. James and Robert returned to Hornby and locked the doors. In the chaos that sprang up, Lord Stanley ordered a giant cannon named Mile Ende, brought up from Bristol, to blast the Harringtons out of Hornby. No shots were fired, and the only explanation appears to be a warrant from the king's youngest brother Richard, Duke of Gloucester, dated 26 March 1470 and signed 'at Hornby'. At seventeen, the duke had chosen a side in the dispute, no doubt believing his brother's decision to be unfair.

Fifteen years later, Lord Stanley would betray Richard, then Richard III, at the Battle of Bosworth. He perhaps remembered how the king, as duke, had taken sides against him in what was to prove a fateful decision.

93. Only One Side in the Wars of the Roses Used a Rose Badge

The Wars of the Roses has traditionally been seen as a thirty-year struggle between the royal Houses of Lancaster and York for the crown of England. The name for the struggle was probably first coined by Sir Walter Scott in his novel *Anne of Geierstein* in 1829. Scott probably based the name on the famous scene in Shakespeare's *Henry VI Part 1* when nobles pick a red or white rose in the Temple Church gardens to show which side they took in the conflict, though in 1762 historian David Hume characterised it as 'the wars between the two roses'.

There is no contemporary evidence that the conflicts were referred to as the Cousins' War either. It seems unlikely that those living through thirty years of sporadic fighting with frequent changes of regime and defections to and from both sides really had a name for what was happening about them. It was just life.

When the first Tudor king took the throne he adopted the Tudor Rose as a badge, a white rose over a red one, as a prominent device of his new dynasty, meaning it to represent the joining of the House of Lancaster, the red rose, with the House of York, the white rose, embodied in his marriage to Edward IV's daughter Elizabeth of York and in their children.

The white rose was among several badges in use by the House of York, though it was not particularly prominent. Richard, Duke of York, had a falcon and fetterlock as a badge, though his son would later use the white rose more widely as Edward IV. The red rose was not a symbol used by the House of Lancaster, at least not by this time. Henry IV may have used it before he became king – one French chronicle, *Traison et Mort*, mentions red roses on

Henry Bolingbroke's tent at a joust in 1398 – but it was not in use by the middle of the century.

During Henry VI's readeption in 1470, the Grocers' Company in London pulled up the white roses they had planted for Edward IV and replaced them with red ones. Henry Tudor was in London at this period and might have seen the symbol before his time in exile. Perhaps it made a mark on him in that brief period beyond its meaning to everyone else at the time.

However it was imagined, the Tudor rose came to symbolise a dynasty and remains a prominent reminder today of a period born out of civil war.

94. The Fate of the Princes in the Tower Remains Unknown

The fate of the Princes in the Tower remains one of history's greatest unanswered and, at present, unanswerable mysteries. They ceased to be seen within the Tower grounds during the summer of 1483 where they had previously been seen playing, but precisely what happened to the twelve-year-old Edward V and his nine-year-old brother Richard of Shrewsbury, Duke of York, has been debated for centuries.

The traditional view is that Richard III ordered the murder of his nephews to secure his throne. In the absence of real evidence, this remains the most likely explanation, but far from the only one. Richard had custody of the boys, yet if he did order their deaths, he left Edward IV's daughters alive and indeed welcomed them to court in 1484 when they emerged from sanctuary. They were no less of a threat, since Henry Tudor had sworn to marry the oldest, Elizabeth of York, to take Richard's throne. Richard's other nephew, George's son Edward and his sister Margaret, were well cared and provided for during Richard's reign, though Edward was surely as much a potential threat as his other nephews, being the son of Richard's older brother. None of these, or any other close relatives, were killed on Richard III's orders, though several would perish at the hands of Tudor kings.

There is a surprising lack of direct evidence against Richard III for the murder of his nephews. No contemporary record names him as their killer. One source from the time discovered in the 1980s among the College of Arms' archives records that the boys were killed 'by the vis of the Duke of Buckingham', though 'vis' could mean advice, implicating Richard, or device, suggesting a plot. Given that Buckingham rebelled in Henry Tudor's name in autumn 1483, the latter is possible. A report by Alvaro Lopes de Chaves, a secretary to the Portuguese king, suggests that the boys were starved or poisoned by Buckingham, as does the Dutch *Devisie Chronicle*.

Following Richard III's death in 1485, there were no direct accusations made against him by Henry VII, Elizabeth Woodville, the boys' mother, or any other source. The politically well-informed *Crowland Chronicle* offers only that as part of Buckingham's Rebellion, 'a rumour was spread that the sons of king Edward before-named had died a violent death, but it was uncertain how', again suggesting Buckingham's involvement but also confirming that there was no more than rumour.

Later, Tudor writers gradually made Richard III the perpetrator. The bones currently resting in the urn in Westminster Abbey are as likely to belong to other bodies as to the Princes in the Tower. Without further testing, which is currently prohibited, that question will also remain unanswered. It also remains possible that one or both of the boys were not murdered in 1483. Perhaps one day, this elusive conundrum will be solved, by science or a chance find in an archive, or perhaps it will remain a mystery.

95. Henry VII Married Elizabeth of York to Heal the Wounds of Civil War

Henry VII became king of England on 22 August 1485 following his victory at the Battle of Bosworth, though his first Parliament, opening on 7 November 1485, dated his reign from 21 August, allowing him to attaint those taking the field with Richard III as traitors. It was a controversial move, since it could deprive Henry himself and future kings of support on the battlefield if men had to be concerned about being attainted for defending the de facto king.

On 10 December, Thomas Lovell, Speaker of the Commons, petitioned the king that he 'should take to himself that illustrious lady Elizabeth, daughter of King Edward IV, as his wife'. Many had followed Henry Tudor to Bosworth because of the promise of a return to Edward IV's line of succession and they were keen to see his oldest daughter married to the new king. Henry was equally concerned that he should not be seen to hold his throne by virtue of his wife, which might explain the slight delay that appeared to be causing concern in the Commons.

It has also been suggested that Henry had heard the rumours about Richard III and his niece from exile and could not be certain of the truth of them. If that was the case, the delay might have been a result of his uncertainty as to whether uncle and niece had been involved in a sexual relationship that could have left Elizabeth pregnant.

The other issue was that Richard III had passed Titulus Regius, making the children of Edward IV illegitimate. If Henry wished to marry Elizabeth, he needed to undo that illegitimacy, but with no clear understanding of the fate of her brothers Edward V and Richard, Duke of York, Henry risked making a rival with a much better claim to the throne and perhaps more support even among his own followers. Although there is no record of an investigation or public proclamation of the fate of the boys, it is inconceivable that Henry did not try to find out what he could quickly. The lack of certain information, even at the time, is perhaps reflected in the fact that even Henry in the attainder passed against Richard III did not accuse him of killing the boys. Titulus Regius was repealed without being read in Parliament and Henry ordered every copy destroyed. The content is only known now because one copy escaped destruction within the papers of Crowland Abbey.

Henry and Elizabeth were married on 18 January 1486 in Westminster Abbey. The couple's first child, Prince Arthur, was born on 20 September 1486 at Winchester, then believed to have been the site of Camelot, offering the promise of a new King Arthur. Elizabeth was crowned on 25 November 1487, over two years after Bosworth, making it clear who was king and that the authority was Henry's, not his wife's.

96. The Battle of Stoke Field Was the Last Pitched Battle of the Wars of the Roses

Henry VII was forced to defend his crown on the battlefield on 16 June 1487 at the Battle of Stoke Field. A Yorkist force had invaded from Ireland, intent on driving Henry from the throne and restoring the House of York.

Two Yorkist figureheads were involved in the invasion. John de la Pole, Earl of Lincoln, was the oldest son of Elizabeth, Duchess of Suffolk, a sister of Edward IV and Richard III. He was the senior male adult heir of the House of York, though his claim came through the female line. The second figurehead was Edward, Earl of Warwick, the son of George, Duke of Clarence, who was an heir in the male line but was only twelve and his father had been attainted. Henry VII believed that he had Edward safely in the Tower of London and paraded the earl to prove as much, but the Yorkist invasion also claimed to have Edward with them, having the boy crowned Edward VI in Dublin before they left Ireland.

The Yorkists were met in Wales by a handful of loyalists, but struggled to gain any more support. They marched to York to appeal for help from Richard III's old heartlands but were refused entry to the city on account of the presence of a large number of Irish kerns, bare-legged, bare-chested soldiers. Heading back south, they were forced to seek a confrontation with King Henry without reinforcements.

On 16 June 1487, Henry put 12,000 men in the field at the command of John de Vere, Earl of Oxford, his trusty general who had helped win Bosworth Field for him. John de la Pole, Earl of Lincoln, commanded the Yorkist force with around 8,000 men. The fighting was reportedly close for sometime with a section of Oxford's men fleeing early, but superior numbers began to tell with the lightly armoured Irish taking the brunt of the casualties. There was a contingent of professional Swiss mercenaries in the Yorkist army under the command of Colonel Martin Schwartz, who fought hard, but Schwartz himself was killed. Lincoln also died in the fighting and Francis, Lord Lovell, a close friend of Richard III, was seen fleeing the field injured and never heard of again.

The twelve-year-old Edward the Yorkists was brought captured and later revealed by the Tudor government to be an imposter named Lambert Simnel from Oxfordshire. Deemed an innocent pawn, Simnel was pardoned by Henry VII and put to work in the royal kitchens, last appearing in the historical record in the mid-1520s as a royal falconer to Henry VIII. His true identity remains a matter heatedly discussed: was he really an imposter, or was Lambert Simnel in fact Edward, Earl of Warwick?

97. Perkin Warbeck's Success Shows That the Wars of the Roses Had Not Ended

Margaret, Dowager Duchess of Burgundy, proved to be a thorn in the side of the new Tudor regime. Margaret was the sister of Edward IV and Richard III who had married Charles the Bold, Duke of Burgundy, in 1468. Charles had died in 1477 but Margaret remained a wealthy and powerful force on the continent. She used every tool at her disposal to try and dislodge Henry VII from his throne.

Margaret had helped the Yorkist invasion of 1487, providing a base of operations and paying for the Swiss mercenaries that accompanied them. In 1490, another boy appeared at the Burgundian court claiming the throne of England, insisting that he was Richard, Duke of York, the younger of the Princes in the Tower. He explained that his older brother Edward V had been murdered on Richard III's orders but that the killers had taken pity on him and smuggled him away to safety.

This new pretender, remembered by history not as Richard, Duke of York, but as Perkin Warbeck, posed a serious threat to Henry VII for almost a decade. Perkin tried to raise support in Ireland in 1491 but found that after their support of Lambert Simnel in 1487 there was little appetite to try again. Returning to the continent, Perkin was welcomed by Charles VIII of France but when Henry VII launched an invasion, Charles quickly offered terms in the Treaty of Etaples, which included the expulsion of Perkin.

Foreign support for Perkin grew. Henry complained to Philip, the new Duke of Burgundy, that he was harbouring the boy but was ignored, causing Henry to cut off trade with Burgundy. The new Holy Roman Emperor Maximilian I (Duke Philip's father) invited Perkin to attend the funeral of the late Holy Roman Emperor Frederick III and recognised the boy as Richard IV. In return, Perkin formally passed his claim to the throne of England to Maximilian if Perkin should die before becoming king.

Perkin sailed for Deal in Kent, another invasion funded by Margaret, but was beaten away without even landing. He moved next to Ireland again and although the Earl of Desmond offered support, Perkin could not get a foothold there either. Things changed when he next moved to Scotland and was well received by James IV. Warbeck married a cousin of the king, Lady Catherine Gordon, and was provided with an army that crossed the border with him in September 1496. Support did not come in the north and the attack was abandoned.

A year later, in September 1497, Warbeck landed in Cornwall within months of a tax revolt there. When a royal army arrived, Perkin panicked and tried to flee but was captured. Initially, surprisingly, welcomed at court, Perkin was nevertheless a prisoner. On 23 November 1499, Perkin was executed for trying to escape from the Tower. The threat he posed demonstrates clearly that no one really knew what had happened to the Princes in the Tower or whether Perkin Warbeck was, in fact, one of them.

98. Edmund de la Pole Was Known as the White Rose

Just before Henry VII's son and heir Prince Arthur was married to Catherine of Aragon in 1501, Edmund and Richard de la Pole fled to the court of Maximilian I, Holy Roman Emperor. Sir Robert Curzon had told Maximilian that England was fed up with Henry's 'murders and tyrannies' and suggested Edmund as an alternative. Maximilian's reported response that he would do all he could to see 'one of Edward's blood' back on the throne probably caused the brothers to make for his court.

Edmund and Richard were younger brothers of John de la Pole, Earl of Lincoln, who had been killed at the Battle of Stoke Field in 1487 as part of Lambert Simnel's invasion. Another brother, Sir William de la Pole, was left behind and quickly arrested and imprisoned. For allowing Edmund de la Pole to pass through Calais, Sir James Tyrell was ordered to submit to arrest. He refused until he and his son were promised safe conduct to the king, only to be arrested as soon as they emerged. Tyrell was tortured in the Tower for information on Edward, though there is no record of him being questioned about the Princes, or that he confessed to involvement in their murder, before he was executed as a traitor a month after the death of Prince Arthur.

Edmund began to openly call himself Duke of Suffolk, his father's title that he had been denied, as well as the White Rose, openly proclaiming his right to Henry's throne. Support was quick to come from King John of Denmark, Sweden and Norway. In 1504, Henry signed a trade deal with the Hanseatic League that was so detrimental to English merchants and the only possible explanation for his agreement lay in the term that the League should offer no support to Edmund de la Pole.

In 1506, Henry had another of his lucky turns of fortune when Maximilian's son Philip was shipwrecked on the English coast. Polydore Virgil wrote that Henry was 'scarcely able to believe his luck when he realized that divine providence had given him the means of getting his hands on Edmund de la Pole, Earl of Suffolk, who had been the leader of the conspiracy against him a few years previously'. Philip was not only forced to sign a trade treaty, but also to promise to give up Edmund de la Pole, insisting that the duke would not be freed until Edmund was in English custody.

Henry promised that Edmund would be pardoned and restored to his lands and titles, but instead he was immediately arrested and thrown in the Tower. On 4 May 1513, Henry's son Henry VIII executed Edmund. Richard took up the mantle of the White Rose and gained support in France but was killed fighting at the Battle of Pavia for France in 1525. William died in 1538, a prisoner in the Tower for thirty-seven years, a record that still stands to this day.

99. Cardinal Reginald Pole Was the Last Yorkist Threat to the Tudor Crown

Reginald Pole was the youngest son of Margaret, Countess of Salisbury, and therefore a grandson of George, Duke of Clarence. Born in 1500 at Stourton Castle near Stourbridge, Reginald embarked on a career in the Church, with Henry VIII contributing to the cost of his education. At twenty-one, Reginald began a six-year period of study at Padua partly funded by Henry. During his time abroad, Reginald met and befriended Erasmus and on his return to England in 1527, appointments and patronage began to flow his way.

Following the death of Cardinal Wolsey, Reginald was offered the Archbishopric of York but refused it, arguing with Henry against the divorce from Catherine of Aragon until the king stormed away, slamming the door behind himself. Reginald left England as the Great Matter escalated. In 1535, he was in Padua again, where he received a letter from Henry VIII asking for his opinion on the divorce, clearly hoping he had paid for an ally in Reginald's training who held increasing sway in Rome.

It took a year for Reginald to formulate his reply, during which the State Papers record a series of letters from Henry asking when the opinion would arrive. What Henry finally received was not a letter, but a book known as De Unitate, or A Defence of the Church's Unity. It was not what Henry had hoped for, but rather a savage rebuttal of Henry's arguments relating to the divorce and a brutal critique of quarter of a century of bad rule and wasteful policy. Reginald's oldest brother Lord Montagu wrote to him slamming the book and the danger it placed the family in. His mother Margaret wrote to him also, referring to 'a terrible message' she had received from Henry.

In 1537, Reginald was created a cardinal without being ordained a priest because papal plots began to revolve around marrying him to Princess Mary and returning the House of York to the throne in union with the House of Tudor. The Pope gave Reginald 10,000 ducats to recruit men in Flanders and Germany and by the end of the year, Henry was offering a reward of 100,000 gold crowns to anyone who brought him Reginald, dead or alive.

The year 1538 saw the arrest, trial and execution of Lord Montagu with Henry Courtenay, Marquis of Exeter. One of Reginald's other brothers, Geoffrey, was arrested and tortured for information on his brothers before Lord Montagu's arrest and tried to take his own life twice during his torture and incarceration. In a further shock, Margaret was executed on 27 May 1541 at the age of sixty-seven.

When Mary became queen, Reginald returned to England and was created Archbishop of Canterbury. He died on 17 November 1558, the very same day as Queen Mary. The last ever Catholic monarch and Archbishop of Canterbury were gone, but so was the last White Rose plot for the throne of England.

100. The Wars of the Roses Was Not a Thirty-Year War for the Crown

The Wars of the Roses is frequently viewed as a thirty-year period of civil war from 1455 to 1485 during which the royal houses of Lancaster and York vied for the throne. In fact, that particular dispute began in 1460 and ended decisively with the extinction of the legitimate House of Lancaster in 1471.

The period known as the Wars of the Roses marked the disintegration of bastard feudalism, a system that allowed great lords to amass personal armies through the scheme of livery and maintenance. This allowed men like the Duke of York and Earl of Warwick to rival the king in power. The weakness of Henry VI, his preference for peace over war, which was considered undesirable at the time, and his later illness all contributed to the dismantling of a system that relied on a firm hand at the very top. Henry could not bring powerful men at odds with each other to terms and so the country slid inexorably towards civil war.

Richard, Duke of York, has been viewed as a power-hungry man who dragged a country into civil war, but the battles came at the end of a long slow spiral that began with support, moved to loyal opposition and finally, when backed into a corner, to war. His primary opponent Edmund, Duke of Somerset, had no power base but had the ear of the king and queen. York had a large power base that made him appear a threat and led to his exclusion. Somerset's weakness became his strength and York's strength became his weakness.

England became aware that an unpopular or unsuccessful monarch could be toppled and when Edward began to distance himself from the Neville family, Warwick was powerful enough to remove him and restore Henry VI, his cause kept alive by Queen Margaret. Remembered as Warwick the Kingmaker, it is a testament to the problems in the structure of late medieval society that a noble could drive a king from his country and these instances must have impacted Henry VII's mistrust of the nobility and the reduction of their influence.

The House of York imploded in 1483, whether for genuine reasons, through the ambition or fear of Richard III or a wider plot in motion to promote Henry Tudor. The disappearance of the Princes in the Tower remains a mystery that divides opinion bitterly today but cannot yet be solved. Richard III might have believed he had more time, but his death at Bosworth left the matter unresolved, ended 331 years of Plantagenet rule and ushered in the Tudor era. Yorkist resistance to Tudor rule persisted well into the reign of Henry VIII and was perhaps only finally extinguished in 1558 with the death of Reginald Pole.

The thirty-year period is perhaps a Tudor construct to portray them as saviours of the nation. Perhaps beginning as early as 1447 and not ending until a century later, national and local feuds kept the embers of war glowing and contributed to one of the longest and most brutal periods of upheaval in English history.